BAPTISTWAYPRESS®

Adult Bible Teaching Guide

Dealing with Hard Times

Job, Ecclesiastes,
Habakkuk,
Lamentations

Vernon Davis
Hollie Atkinson
Stephen Von Wyrick
Bruce Cresson
Larry Shotwell
Robby Barrett
Liz Laughlin
Donovan Fredricksen

BAPTISTWAYPRESS®

Dallas, Texas

BAPTISTWAY PRESS® Management Team
Executive Director, Baptist General Convention of Texas: Charles Wade
Director, Missions, Evangelism, and Ministry Team: Wayne Shuffield
Ministry Team Leader: Phil Miller
Publisher, BAPTISTWAY PRESS®: Ross West

Cover and Interior Design and Production: Desktop Miracles, Inc.
Printing: Data Reproductions Corporation
Cover Photo: Oasis near the Dead Sea, iStockphoto.com

First edition: June 2007
ISBN 1–931060–92–4

How to Make the Best Use of This Teaching Guide

Leading a class in studying the Bible is a sacred trust. This *Teaching Guide* has been prepared to help you as you give your best to this important task.

In each lesson, you will find first "Bible Comments" for teachers, to aid you in your study and preparation. The three sections of "Bible Comments" are "Understanding the Context," "Interpreting the Scriptures," and "Focusing on the Meaning." "Understanding the Context" provides a summary overview of the entire background passage that also sets the passage in the context of the Bible book being studied. "Interpreting the Scriptures" provides verse-by-verse comments on the focal passage. "Focusing on the Meaning" offers help with the meaning and application of the focal text.

The second main part of each lesson is "Teaching Plans." You'll find two complete teaching plans in this section. The first is called "Teaching Plan—Varied Learning Activities," and the second is called "Teaching Plan—Lecture and Questions." Choose the plan that best fits your class and your style of teaching. You may also use and adapt ideas from both. Each plan is intended to be practical, helpful, and immediately useful as you prepare to teach.

The major headings in each teaching plan are intended to help you sequence how you teach so as to follow the flow of how people tend to learn. The first major heading, "Connect with Life," provides ideas that will help you begin the class session where your class is and draw your class into the study. The second major heading, "Guide Bible Study," offers suggestions for helping your class engage the Scriptures actively and develop a greater understanding of this portion of the Bible's message. The third major heading, "Encourage Application," is meant to help participants focus on how to respond with their lives to this message.

As you and your class begin the study, take time to lead them in writing the date on which each lesson will be studied on the first page of each lesson and/or on the contents page of the *Study Guide.* You may also find it helpful to make and post a chart that indicates the date on which each lesson will be studied. If all of your class has e-mail, send them an e-mail with the dates the lessons will be studied. (At least one church that uses BAPTISTWAY® materials for its classes places a sticker on the table of contents to identify the dates.)

Here are some steps you can take to help you prepare well to teach each lesson and save time in doing so:

1. Start early in the week before your class meets.

2. If your church's adult Bible study teachers meet for lesson overview and preparation, plan to participate. If your church's adult Bible study teachers don't have this planning time now, look for ways to begin. You, your fellow teachers, and your church will benefit from this mutual encouragement and preparation.

3. Overview the study in the *Study Guide*. Look at the table of contents, and see where this lesson fits in the overall study. Then read or review the study introduction to the book that is being studied.

4. Consider carefully the suggested Main Idea, Question to Explore, and Teaching Aim. These can help you discover the main thrust of this particular lesson.

5. Use your Bible to read and consider prayerfully the Scripture passages for the lesson. Using your Bible in your study and in the class session can provide a positive model to class members to use their own Bibles and give more attention to Bible study themselves. (Each writer of the Bible comments in both the *Teaching Guide* and the *Study Guide* has chosen a favorite translation. You're free to use the Bible translation you prefer and compare it with the translations chosen, of course.)

6. After reading all the Scripture passages in your Bible, then read the Bible comments in the *Study Guide*. The Bible comments are intended to be an aid to your study of the Bible. Read also the small articles—"sidebars"—in each lesson. They are intended to provide additional, enrichment information and inspiration and to encourage thought and application. Try to answer for yourself the questions included in each lesson. They're intended to encourage further thought and application, and you can also use them in the class session itself. Continue your Bible study with the aid of the Bible comments included in this *Teaching Guide*.

7. Review the "Teaching Plans" in this *Teaching Guide.* Consider how these suggestions would help you teach this Bible passage in your class to accomplish the teaching aim.

8. Consider prayerfully the needs of your class, and think about how to teach so you can help your class learn best.

9. Develop and follow a lesson plan based on the suggestions in this *Teaching Guide,* with alterations as needed for your class.

10. Enjoy leading your class in discovering the meaning of the Scripture passages and in applying these passages to their lives.

FREE! Additional adult Bible study comments by Dr. Jim Denison, pastor of Park Cities Baptist Church, Dallas, Texas, are online at www.baptistwaypress.org and can be downloaded free. These lessons are posted on the internet a week in advance of the first Sunday of use.

FREE! Downloadable teaching resource items for use in your class are available at www.baptistwaypress.org! Watch for them in "Teaching Plans" for each lesson. Then go online to www.baptistwaypress.org and click on "Teaching Resource Items" for this study. These items are selected from "Teaching Plans." They are provided online to make lesson preparation easier for hand-outs and similar items. Permission is granted to download these teaching resource items, print them out, copy them as needed, and use them in your class.

ALSO FREE! An additional teaching plan is available each week at www.baptistwaypress.org.

IN ADDITION: Enrichment teaching help is provided in the internet edition of the *Baptist Standard.* Access the *FREE* internet information by checking the *Baptist Standard* website at www.baptiststandard.com. Call 214–630–4571 to begin your subscription to the printed edition of the *Baptist Standard.*

Writers for This Teaching Guide

Vernon Davis, writer of "Bible Comments" for lessons 1–6 on Job, is retired as dean of the Logsdon School of Theology, Hardin-Simmons University, Abilene, Texas. Dr. Davis has also served as pastor of First Baptist Church, Alexandria, Virginia, and as professor and dean at Midwestern Baptist Theological Seminary, Kansas City, Missouri.

Larry Shotwell, writer of "Teaching Plans" for lessons 1–6 on Job, is pastor's visitation assistant at First Baptist Church, San Angelo, Texas. He is a veteran writer of teaching plans and many other materials. He served formerly as manager of the Adult Sunday School Program Section at LifeWay Christian Resources, Nashville, Tennessee.

Hollie Atkinson wrote "Bible Comments" for lessons 7–9 on Ecclesiastes. Dr. Atkinson lives in Georgetown, Texas, and is retired after serving as pastor and teaching and ministering on university campuses.

Robby Barrett wrote "Teaching Plans" for lessons 7–9 on Ecclesiastes. Robby is minister of education at First Baptist Church, Amarillo, Texas. He has written numerous teaching plans for BAPTISTWAY®.

Stephen Von Wyrick, Ph.D., wrote "Bible Comments" for lessons 10–11 on Habakkuk. He serves as professor of Hebrew Bible and Archaeology at the University of Mary Hardin-Baylor and as a lecturer in religion at Baylor University.

Liz Laughlin, writer of "Teaching Plans" for lessons 10–11 on Habakkuk, is minister with singles and senior adults and church pianist at First Baptist Church, San Angelo, Texas. She is involved in missions around the world, and most recently spent two weeks on a boat in the Peruvian Amazon on a medical missions trip.

Bruce Cresson wrote "Bible Comments" for lessons 12–13 on Lamentations. Dr. Cresson is retired as professor of religion at Baylor University. He teaches a Bible study class at Columbus Avenue Baptist Church, Waco, Texas.

Donovan Fredricksen wrote "Teaching Plans" for lessons 12–13 on Lamentations. Dr. Fredricksen is dean of the College of Adult Education at Dallas Baptist University, Dallas, Texas. He earned a B.B.A. in accounting from Texas Wesleyan University, and an M.R.E. and Ph.D. from Southwestern Baptist Theological Seminary.

Dealing with Hard Times:
Job, Ecclesiastes, Habakkuk, Lamentations

Focal Text
Job 1:1; 1:6—2:10

Background
Job 1:1—2:10

Main Idea
Job's suffering was not what would have been expected to happen to a person who was righteous.

Question to Explore
Does righteous living provide insurance against bad things happening to us?

Teaching Aim
To lead participants to summarize the story of Job and state implications for the questions it raises about suffering

JOB

God and Suffering

Lesson One

When Bad Things Happen to a Good Person

BIBLE COMMENTS

Understanding the Context

Suffering that seems undeserved or out of proportion to its known cause inevitably raises profound personal religious issues. Such suffering tests the truth of our common assumptions about God's ways with human beings and can even threaten the reality of our relationship with God. Suffering can become an experience that draws us into the light of deeper faith or that thrusts us into the dark night of cynicism and despair. It affects our thoughts and our prayers, our wisdom and our worship.

The Book of Job wrestles with the persistent problem of the meaning of personal suffering. The book is based on the experience of the man Job, well known in Jewish tradition for his remarkable faith and personal integrity (see Ezekiel 14:12–20). His story intensifies the issue of the meaning of suffering, for in Job the most terrible things imaginable happen to the finest person one could know. The story thus casts the problem in its most extreme form.

The prose narrative of the book (Job 1:1—2:13; 42:7–17) presents Job's suffering as a test of his motives for faith. Would Job's faith be real if it were not rewarded? The drama of Job turns on this question: *Is there a faith in God that is genuine, one that is independent of our affluence or poverty and not threatened by our pleasure or pain?* The risk of God, the test of Satan (the Accuser), and the response of Job all seek the answer. Clearly, Job was unaware of the heavenly agreement between God and the Accuser that lay behind his crisis of faith.

The prose narrative affirms the faithfulness of Job in spite of his suffering and the enormity of his loss. His reputation for patience has come from this section. The prose story relates the successful outcome of his crisis without revealing Job's internal struggle and his later honest confrontation with God and his friends about his plight. Yet, to know Job's patience without acknowledging his protests and to accept his affirmations without seeing his agonizing struggle is to have only a superficial knowledge of the man. Many people today readily identify with Job's struggle to find meaning and his search for the reality of God in hard times.

The prolonged struggle of Job emerges clearly in the poetic monologues and dialogues that comprise the heart of the book. These passages are difficult to interpret because they employ ancient poetic imagery and unfamiliar theological argument. The speeches are repetitive, and they often seem to reason in a circle. They are challenging primarily, however, because they grapple with a universal human problem that has defied easy answers and intellectual solutions that are completely satisfying.

Interpreting the Scriptures

Pious and Prosperous (1:1–5)

The prologue makes clear Job was a person of integrity, "blameless and upright" (1:1).[1] His faith was genuine and his conduct above reproach. His motives were sound and his actions transparent. Job should not be understood as self-righteous or concerned merely with ritual correctness. In his extended speech in Job 31:5–35, he testified that his blameless life included more than avoiding evil. He lived with integrity and with a compassion for others that moved him to address injustice.

Job "feared God and turned away from evil" (1:1). The wisdom literature of Israel often refers to the fear of God as the beginning of wisdom and the heart of true religious commitment (see Proverbs 1:7). To fear God was to hold God in reverential awe and respond to God in obedience. Linking the fear of God and turning from evil reflects the biblical connection between belief and behavior, the profession and the practice of faith. One's relationship with God provides both the means and the motivation for turning away from evil.

The wisdom of ancient Israel linked piety and prosperity. Common tradition held that the righteous would prosper, and prosperity was most often measured by the size of one's herds and the number of one's children. By all counts Job was a prosperous man, and his culture and theology saw this as indisputable evidence of God's blessing on him.

Job provided for his family materially, but he was also concerned for their spiritual welfare. Job 1:4–5 depicts Job's acting as priest for his family, a common practice in patriarchal times. The close relationship among Job's children can be seen in their frequent celebrations and feasts. Job feared these celebrations might have resulted in excess and sinful behavior. He was concerned to "sanctify" his children, which probably involved a ritual of cleansing or purification to prepare them for offering sacrifices to God. Job's consistency in these matters is noted in the words: "This is what Job always did" (Job 1:5). Faithfulness is not genetically passed from one generation to the next, however. Job could offer sacrifices for others but could not ensure they would accept his values or follow his example.

Testing the Motive of Faith (1:6–12)

The Book of Job presents his story through alternating scenes that take place both on earth and in the setting of a heavenly council. From the initial meeting of the heavenly council, one can reach two basic conclusions. First, neither Job nor the other speakers on earth had access to the charges made against him or the agreement of God to allow his suffering. Second, the narrative sees the suffering of Job as being a test of his faith rather than a punishment for his sin. The later speeches of Job and his friends that comprise the body of the book probe the question of whether Job's sin was the primary reason for his suffering.

The heavenly scene pictures God in the likeness of an ancient eastern ruler with his royal court arrayed before him. The "heavenly beings" (1:6), or literally "the sons of God," who make up this assembly have different functions in the work of the kingdom. Some interpreters refer to them as a heavenly court of angels or messengers. In this particular session only one is identified by function. "Satan" is literally translated *the accuser* or *the adversary*. He is portrayed as a kind of royal prosecutor responsible for searching for those who had committed wrongs and bringing them to account. He is not depicted in this text as a fallen angel or as the being who would come to be fully understood as the evil one or the devil in later Judaism and the New Testament.

In response to the Lord's inquiry concerning his activities, Satan replied that he had been going about his business on earth, but he gave no specific example of what he had done. The Lord asked: "Have you considered my servant Job?" (1:8). Literally, *Have you set your heart upon my servant Job?* The Lord expressed his unconditional confidence in the uniqueness of Job's commitment and character. The Lord's reference to Job as "my servant" placed him among other notable Old Testament figures—patriarchs, kings, and prophets. The Lord then reaffirmed the description of Job given at the beginning of the book.

Satan questioned the motivation that lay behind Job's piety. He posed the question many see as the book's central issue: "Does Job fear God for nothing?" (1:9). Did Job serve God because of who God is or only because of the benefits that came from being faithful? Satan believed self-interest lay at the heart of Job's religion, and he challenged God to remove his blessing and protection from Job to see whether the motivation of his faith were genuine. The scene closes with the Lord's acceptance of Satan's challenge. He granted Satan the permission to strip Job of all that he had, with the limitation that he could not bring him physical harm (1:12).

When Life Tumbles In (1:13–22)

In the aftermath of the heavenly council, Job experienced a tidal wave of misfortune. A succession of events stripped all his possessions from him and brought death to his servants and his sons and daughters. Note that the immediate causes of these catastrophes were both the evil actions of humans and natural phenomena. Job's faith and tradition, however, did not focus on what we see as immediate causes. He understood all that happened to be caused or permitted by God, who was in control of everything. Note especially that he did not even assess blame for these events to Satan.

Job's response to his devastating personal loss was not what Satan had predicted. He did not turn away from God; instead, he worshiped God (1:20–21). He "tore his robe" and "shaved his head," which were traditional symbolic expressions in a ritual of grief for one in mourning. He did not rage against heaven, but rather he "fell on the ground," an expression of humility and submission to God.

JOB: God and Suffering

Job's words express his personal acceptance of all that had happened to him as coming from God. They convey his belief that his life and all that he possessed were gifts from God. The meaning of his life was not in these things but in the reality of his faith in God. Job's words, "the Lord gave and the Lord has taken away" (1:21), may have been an ancient liturgical blessing to express his praise to God even in the experience of great loss.

"In all this Job did not sin" (1:22). The relationship between sin and suffering is complex. Although sin, turning against God and God's will, brings inevitable consequences that include suffering, one cannot conclude that all suffering therefore comes as a result of one's sin. Job's experience is the classic example of this truth. One may suffer because of the sin of others or because of the condition of the prevailing culture. One may suffer because of natural disasters or seemingly random and accidental events. Clearly, however, the experience of suffering may become the occasion for one's sin. In suffering a person may turn against God and others. Suffering may result in making decisions based on expediency, to ease our pain at the expense of our integrity. Even though Job experienced overwhelming loss, which he could not understand and which he would not forever bear in silence, he continued to affirm his faith and live in obedience to God.

A Second Testing (2:1–10)

Job's experience demonstrates that the testing of our faith is never finished. New commitments bring new challenges, often more intense than any we have faced before. Our past record of resistance to temptation may strengthen us for new trials, but it does not ensure we will be able to overcome them.

In many respects the second chapter of Job is parallel to the first. The Lord affirmed Job in the same terms used in the first encounter. Then, he added that Job "still persists in his integrity" (2:3). The word for "integrity," or *wholeness*, is translated "blameless" in the earlier reference to Job's character (1:1). The Lord charged Satan with attempting to destroy Job "for no reason" (2:3). His accusations had been baseless.

In the first test Satan charged that Job served God only because it was a way to self-aggrandizement. In the second test Satan assumed that Job served God only because it was the way to self-preservation. "All that people have they will give to save their lives" (2:4). The Lord disagreed but permitted Satan's further testing, with the condition that Job's life be spared.

Lesson 1: When Bad Things Happen to a Good Person

The ensuing suffering of Job involved a most repulsive condition, as sores or boils covered his body. His pain was excruciating; and he also experienced the unwelcome challenge of his wife's taunt: "Curse God and die" (2:9). In all of this, however, Job reaffirmed his faith in God and his expectation that he would receive both good and bad at the hand of God. As in the first testing, the scene closes with the affirmation that Job's suffering did not become the occasion of his sin.

Focusing on the Meaning

People often want to measure the results of faith in material terms. When we read that Job was "blameless and upright, one who feared God and turned away from evil" (1:1), we find it easy to believe that he was also materially blessed. It made sense to say to an affluent Job, *You must be living right!* But how could you explain Job's trouble if his religion were real? If faith produces success, its value seems obvious. But what is the worth of faith when it results in suffering rather than material rewards?

Job's story acknowledges that people may do the right thing for the wrong reason. People may avow faith in God because they see this as a way to prosper materially or to achieve social status. Trouble can become a testing ground for the reality of our faith. Job in his loss demonstrated there is such a thing as the unbribed worship of God. For many, however, hard times may reveal that they will *not* "fear God for nothing" (1:9).

How can one find the way to remain faithful in the experience of suffering and loss? Job reminded himself of the gains he had experienced as well as the losses. He placed his suffering in perspective by remembering the blessings of life as well as the suffering. His affirmations in 1:21 and 2:10 reveal a person who knew the therapy of thanksgiving and received life as a gift.

Job's trials demonstrate that to turn away from God in an attempt to find a more satisfying intellectual explanation of suffering is to turn away from the source of the ultimate solution of the problem. Ultimately, the solution to Job's problem of suffering would not be discovered in any explanation of it but rather in the deeper relationship with God he came to experience because of it.

TEACHING PLANS

Teaching Plan—Varied Learning Activities

Connect with Life

1. Make sure everyone has a copy of the *Study Guide*. Lead the class to look at the list of lessons on the contents page and to write in the date each lesson will be studied. List these dates on the marker-board or a poster in advance. (Some classes distribute bookmarks with the dates and lessons listed. Others use e-mail or stickers placed on the *Study Guide* to identify the dates of study.) Guide the class to consider the four units of study and how they relate, underlining significant ideas in the introductory article, "Introducing Dealing with Hard Times: Job, Ecclesiastes, Habakkuk, Lamentations."

2. In advance, ask a class member who enjoys doing research to prepare a two-minute report on the ideas about date and authorship of the Book of Job. After the report has been presented, ask the class to read paragraph three in the introductory article titled "Introducing Job: God and Suffering." The paragraph begins, "Job is part of the wisdom literature. . . ." Refer to the Question to Explore for lesson one: "Does righteous living provide insurance against bad things happening to us?"

Guide Bible Study

3. Ask participants to work in pairs to complete the following handout. (Download at www.baptistwaypress.org.)

What Do You Know About Job?

Check all of the sentences you think are correct about Job.
____ a. Job was a person of great wealth.
____ b. Job lived in the same place that was later visited by a girl named Dorothy.
____ c. Job was a man who never sinned.

LESSON 1: When Bad Things Happen to a Good Person

___ d. Job was the greatest man of all the people in the east.

___ e. Job feared God and turned away from evil.

___ f. Job had seven daughters and three sons.

___ g. Job was described as "no one like him in all the earth."

___ h. Job believed that he prospered because God blessed righteous people.

___ i. Job was a patient man.

Review the answers and use the responses to lead a discussion of the attributes of Job found in Job 1:1–5.

4. Prepare in advance a script for a dramatic reading of the focal verses for this lesson (download at www.baptistwaypress.org). Enlist readers who will read the following parts: Narrator, The Lord, Satan, Messenger 1, Messenger 2, Messenger 3, Messenger 4, Job, and Job's wife. If the class is small, readers could be assigned more than one part or the four messenger parts could be combined. Ask the class to listen for the events of the story as the reading is presented.

5. Read and discuss the *Study Guide* article titled "Satan" to consider one explanation about Satan being a part of the heavenly beings that have access to God. If class members bring Bibles representing various translations, invite them to share different ways Job 1:6 is translated. Ask, *What does Job 1:7 suggest about Satan's activity in the world then and now?* Read Job 1:9, and point out the significance of Satan's question in light of the overall study. Ask the class to respond to question 3 at the end of the lesson in the *Study Guide*.

6. Write "What Job Lost" at the top of the markerboard, and ask the class to search Job 1:13–19 to find what the messengers told Job about his losses. List these losses on the board as they are shared. Read Job 1:20–21 and discuss Job's reaction to his losses. Encourage the class to scan Job 2:1–8. Guide the class to discuss responses to the following questions:
   • How might people today react to such losses?
   • What are some differences in the way Christians and non-Christians might deal with such losses?
   • How might people react differently when faced with personal physical problems?

- What do these Scripture passages reveal about Job's grief?
- What lessons from this passage could Christian people learn about grief when they experience losses related to possessions, family, and health?

7. Lead the class to look at Job 2:9–10 and discuss possible reasons Job's wife advised Job to "Curse God, and die." Ask, *How does Job's reaction reveal Job's belief that all experiences, good and bad, are the result of God's justice? What are some examples that suggest some people still believe this way?*

Encourage Application

8. On the reverse side of the handout distributed in step 3, print "Implications about Suffering" from this Bible passage. (Download at www.baptistwaypress.org.)

Implications About Suffering

_____ Suffering is experienced by both believers and non-believers.

_____ God sometimes allows suffering to test a believer's faith.

_____ Suffering sometimes forces believers to test their convictions and mature in their faith.

_____ To be human and to live in this world with other people is to be exposed to suffering and pain.

_____ While all evil and sin have consequences, not all suffering is the consequence of sin.

_____ Grief is a normal emotion that can be a healthy way to deal with suffering.

Encourage everyone to read the list and select at least two implications that have special meaning. Discuss these implications as members share the statements chosen. Close with prayer for people who are suffering today.

Teaching Plan—Lecture and Questions

Connect with Life

1. Make sure everyone has a *Study Guide*. Before class write the dates for each lesson on the markerboard or a poster, and ask everyone to date the lessons on the contents page. (See step 1, "Teaching Plan—Varied Learning Activities," for other ideas for helping class members be aware of the dates the lessons will be studied.) Bring to class four or five clippings from recent newspapers containing stories about tragic events in the lives of people. Point out that the study of Job will help the class answer questions about tragedies that occur in the lives of both righteous and unrighteous people. Review some of the content in the introductory article titled "Introducing Dealing with Hard Times: Job, Ecclesiastes, Habakkuk, Lamentations." Ask members to underline significant ideas in the article.

Guide Bible Study

2. Present a short lecture about the Book of Job using "Introducing Job: God and Suffering" in the *Study Guide* and introductory information in "Bible Comments" in this *Teaching Guide*. Give special attention to the popular religious belief of the day that suffering was the result of sin. Ask, *What are some examples that this belief is still prevalent today?* Post the outline of the lesson on the focal wall as follows:

When Bad Things Happen to a Good Person
A Man Named Job (1:1)
Testing, Testing (1:6—2:10)

---

3. Read Job 1:1. If you have a map, point out a possible location of the land of Uz. Refer to Lamentations 4:21 as a possible way to identify this location (associated with Edom). List other facts about Job as given in Job 1:2–5.

4. Enlist a volunteer to read Job 1:6–12. Ask the class to look at the short article in the *Study Guide* titled "Satan." Review this article

to present at least one idea for why Satan was a part of the heavenly beings. Lecture briefly on the significance of the question Satan asked in verse 9, "Does Job fear God for nothing?" Lead the class to respond to question 3 at the end of the lesson in the *Study Guide.*

5. Instruct the class to listen for Job's tragic losses as a volunteer reads Job 1:13–19. Invite another volunteer to read Job 2:1–9. On the markerboard, write "Possessions," "Family," "Other." After the readings, ask participants to mention what Job lost. List the responses under the headings.

6. Read Job 1:20–22 and 2:10 to show how Job handled his losses. Ask, *How might other people respond?*

Encourage Application

7. Use the suggestions in the *Study Guide* titled "Practical Insights from Job's Experience" and the small article "Applying the Experience of Job" to state some implications for the questions this story raises about suffering. Consider evaluating the "Implications About Suffering" in step 8 of the other teaching plan. Invite participants to share thoughts and experiences they or their acquaintances have had related to suffering. Allow the class to share the names of people who are suffering, and close with a prayer for them.

NOTES

1. Unless otherwise indicated, all Scripture quotes in lessons 1–6 on Job are from the New Revised Standard Version.

LESSON 1: When Bad Things Happen to a Good Person

Job 3

Job 2:11—3:26

Main Idea

When people are
in the depths of
suffering, it is easy to
be overcome by despair
at what is happening
and question why.

**Question to
Explore**

When suffering comes,
what will we do?

Teaching Aim

To lead participants to
describe and evaluate
Job's agonized response
to his suffering in light of
people's suffering today

JOB

God and Suffering

Lesson Two

The Agony of Why

BIBLE COMMENTS

Understanding the Context

Job bore his suffering with dignity and refrained
from turning away from God. Yet, he would
not continue to suffer in silence and isolation
from others. His suffering persisted and in time
became widely known. Having heard of Job's
plight, three friends came from distant places to
console him. The time that elapsed between the
onslaught of Job's trouble and the arrival of these
friends cannot be determined precisely.

When Job's friends arrived, they found him
still engaged in his extended ritual of grief. Sitting among the ashes in torn clothing, he endured
the relentless pain that had disfigured his coun-
tenance beyond their recognition. They shared
in the ritual of grief and sat with him without
speaking for seven days and nights. Then, Job
broke the silence.

The impassioned speech of Job introduces the
cycles of dialogue that form the body of the book.
The speeches, in contrast to the narrative introduction, are in poetic form. Although spoken
in the presence of his friends, Job's words are a
soliloquy that does not directly address either
them or God. They reveal the depth of the distress that had simmered unspoken within Job's

22

troubled spirit. To no one in particular he vented his bitterness and voiced his despair. Job's speech contains many of the basic characteristics of a lament, a form of outcry found frequently in the Old Testament, especially in the Psalms. Note typical examples in Psalms 22 and 88.

Most often the laments recorded in the Bible come from one who has suffered great loss or experienced a perceived injustice. The injury may be personal, as in the case of Job, or it could be the plight of the people of God, to which an individual gives response. The lament is the expression of honest speech unfiltered by concern for cultural correctness or theological restraint. The lament, usually addressed to God, is an outcry that takes the form of prayer.

The lament expresses pain and protest. Although a cry of near despair, the lament does not turn away from God but rather sees God as the only source of relief. The lament typically contains a catalogue of troubles and a notable absence of the recognition of anything good.

Suffering has the power to distort one's perception of life, magnifying one's personal pain and minimizing the problems of others. It focuses on the misery of the present and forgets the mercy of the past. In lament a person senses disconnection from God, and this intensifies the pain of isolation and the loss of hope. Laments demand explanation for one's trouble and express the desire for retribution. They seek judgment on one's enemies and restoration of life to its good state.

Interpreting the Scriptures

Cursing the Darkness (3:1–10)

3:1. Job "cursed the day of his birth." A curse was a strong expression of a person's wish that evil come upon another. Ancient people believed the spoken word, especially in worship or formal settings, had a life of its own and the power to fulfill itself. Here, Job directed the curse to his own life and decried his own existence. The word used here for "cursed" conveys the idea of *to make meaningless.*

3:2–10. The content of Job's curse on his life is in thirteen statements that begin with the word "let." The cumulative effect of these statements is to denounce the day of his birth and any announcement made of it. Although blotting the day from the calendar could not realistically happen, these statements make clear the depth of despair Job felt about his life and his wish that he had never been born.

The repetitive use of images of darkness is typical of laments. Note how frequently terms such as "darkness," "gloom," and "clouds" appear in this section. In contrast to the dawning of the light, Job called for the darkness to overcome the light and block out any evidence of his existence.

Job 3:8 speaks of those "who curse the Sea." Be aware that other versions translate the Hebrew word here translated "Sea" as "day" (NIV, NASB, KJV, RSV). In Job's desire to blot out the day of his birth, he called for help from people who were known to be effective in pronouncing curses. For the Hebrews, who were not seagoing people, the image of the sea was often used as a symbol of turmoil and trouble. Note that centuries later, when the writer of the Book of Revelation described his vision of the new heaven and new earth, he said that "the sea was no more" (Revelation 21:1).

"Leviathan" was known in ancient Semitic thought as a sea monster that was responsible for chaos and opposed to order. According to this understanding, God subdued Leviathan in creation, bringing order out of chaos. The reference here reflects Job's wish that primeval chaos had prevailed and the created order had been disrupted before he was born. See other references to Leviathan in Psalm 74:12–14; Isaiah 27:1 (see also Job 41:1).

Searching for Answers (3:11–19)

The dominant word in Job's cluster of curses was "let," as he expressed his strong yet unrealistic desire that history be reversed and that he had never been born. As his soliloquy continued, the dominant word became "why." Job turned from cursing the darkness to an agonizing search for answers to his probing questions concerning the meaning of his life. He asked whether it would not have been better for him to have died at birth.

3:12. The image of "knees to receive me" may refer to the knees of his mother or of a midwife. But it likely refers to the custom in that day of the father taking the infant on his lap, and in that act accepting the child as legitimate. Job questioned why he had a father and mother to start him on the life that ultimately resulted in misery.

3:13–19. The Old Testament has a limited development of ideas concerning life after death. These verses provide unique insight into how Job understood *sheol*, the realm of the dead. Most of the references in other

Old Testament books depict *sheol* in far less positive terms. In the grip of his suffering, Job came to a distorted view of what his existence could have been had he died at birth. He saw *sheol* as a place of rest and quietness. Those who were there were removed from the trouble caused by evil people and the injustices of this life. Job saw the life beyond as one in which inequities that characterize the present time would be abolished. He described death as the great liberator. There the small and great, slaves and masters, existed together in a state of peaceful equality. Contrast this grand vision with Job's description of his present experience of suffering: "I am not at ease, nor am I quiet. I have no rest; but trouble comes" (Job 3:26).

Longing for Death (3:20–26)

Job did not question the value of life for everyone, but only for himself. The suffering, which he could not understand, had robbed his life of its meaning and purpose. The tradition of Israel saw death as an enemy, but the despondent Job looked on it as a friend. In much of the Old Testament, death is understood as defeat, but Job looked to it as release.

3:20. Job's misery had made him "bitter in soul." All that had happened to him resulted in an attitude of deep and powerful resentment within him. Until this point Job had not given full expression to his thoughts and feelings. The longer he suffered in silence, though, the more his bitterness simmered inside him.

3:21–22. Job identified himself as one of those who "long for death, but it does not come." He compared his quest to one who searches for hidden treasure and finally discovers it. Job expressed intense frustration that he could not die, but he gave no indication that he attempted to do anything to bring about his death. He continued to believe that "the LORD gave, and the LORD has taken away" (2:21), and he left the matter in the hands of God. Suffering can become so intense and pervasive that it distorts a person's view of life and blinds one to the good alternatives that may be accessible.

A person in the depth of despair that Job experienced is at a danger point in life and should not face it alone. A caring friend, a trusted counselor, or a spiritual guide can provide perspective and support that one can rely on in making the journey out of the dark night of the soul. Unfortunately, Job's friends, although well-intentioned, were not able to understand his need fully or be of much if any help.

3:23. In this statement Job appears to attribute responsibility for his suffering to God for the first time. He "cannot see the way," for God has "fenced" him in. Job felt trapped with no way to escape. The dialogues that follow in the book make Job's confrontations with God more direct and pointed. Here, however, Job acknowledged that he had no hope and could do nothing about it.

A sense of hopelessness is the most difficult aspect of suffering one can experience. In the beginning of the testing of Job, the Accuser complained to God that God had built a "fence" around Job, protecting him from trouble and loss (1:10). In a quite different use of the image, Job spoke of experiencing God's fencing not as protection but as imprisonment.

3:24–26. The closing words of Job's lament describe his suffering as all-consuming. He knew no relief from his torment. The references to "bread" and "water" may indicate that even the most mundane things of his life were accomplished with great effort and intense pain. Sores covered his body and made it difficult for him to take nourishment or quench his thirst. Job also noted an additional dimension of his suffering—the fear that gripped him. What he most feared had come to pass, and he lived with the dread of what would happen next. He was convinced that more trouble would come.

Focusing on the Meaning

What can you do when your life is engulfed by trouble you find impossible to understand and difficult to accept? What can we learn from Job, especially from the words of his lament that poured out in pain and protest? Perhaps there are both positive and negative insights that could come for people who suffer today.

1. Job's response demonstrates the value of honest expression of one's deepest feelings to God and others in times of personal crisis. When we find our inner voice to bring before God what is really going on with us at the depth of life, we are experiencing reality in prayer. Too often we edit our prayers before we offer them. Being overly concerned to say the right things in the right way, we may fail to be honest with God. Poet and hymn writer James Montgomery (1771–1854) wrote:

Prayer is the soul's sincere desire, unuttered or expressed;
The motion of a hidden fire that trembles in the breast.

Questions that we stifle and pain we deny do not merely go away. They can fester and damage our relationship with God and others. They may finally explode in anger or bring us to experience serious depression.

2. When suffering comes, we can find value in putting our problems into words and finding ways to name the darkness that envelops us. The process itself can help drain our emotions and enable us to discover accessible alternatives. For many people, writing becomes a helpful way of dealing with personal pain. Looking at one's anger and despair in black-and-white words on a page may help a person focus thoughts and discover ways to act or pray. The angry, unmailed letter, crumpled and tossed in the waste basket, and the reflective thoughts written in one's personal journal may alike be helpful in dealing with private pain.

3. Although we may find momentary relief in simply venting our anger and frustration, we may also run the risk of becoming preoccupied by our pain. We may get caught in a downward spiral of self-pity and cynicism. Laments can become an excessive litany of protest and repetitive recital of our pain.

4. In lament there is the risk of becoming focused on words at the expense of action. In a study group on the Book of Job, one person observed: "Nobody does anything in Job but talk!" He was making the point that sometimes in the experience of loss and suffering, it is helpful to find something to do. In suffering we may find that our world tends to shrink to the dimensions of our own pain. Only with great effort can we think of the needs of someone else; but that may become the most helpful thing we can do.

A young woman in the grip of depression found nothing meaningful or positive and at times despaired of life itself. In a series of pastoral conversations, her minister searched for something that might arouse a glimmer of interest in life outside herself. After several weeks, the minister encouraged her to volunteer to help with a weekday program for children in the church's mission center. Reluctantly, she agreed to try. After two weeks, she missed an appointment with the minister, but she slipped a note under the minister's office door. The note read: "I've learned to give myself to people who have it worse than I do. If I'm good for them, perhaps I'm not bad for myself."

TEACHING PLANS

Teaching Plan—Varied Learning Activities

Connect with Life

1. Cut apart the life situations listed below, and distribute them to members as they arrive. Ask members to read the statements when requested. Be sensitive to the needs of the members who are enlisted, and avoid asking anyone to read a situation that is similar to one he or she has experienced. (Download at www.baptistwaypress.org.)

Life Situations

(1) I thought my marriage was okay, but my husband (wife) found someone else and divorced me. Why did this happen to me?

(2) My fifteen-year-old son was in a boating accident and drowned. God, why did you take him away from me?

(3) We had just finished our dream home when everything we owned was destroyed in a flood. Why?

(4) My daughter ran away from home and got involved with drugs and prostitution. Why did she do this to me?

(5) I was diagnosed with cancer, and the doctor says I have only a short time to live. Why is my life being cut short?

(6) Our world is in a big mess right now. Why can't we have peace?

Invite the class to share other situations that cause people to ask *why*. Make the transition into the Bible study by sharing that Job also asked *why* when confronted with his trials.

Guide Bible Study

2. Read Job 2:11–13, and ask the class to listen for positive actions Job's friends did. Call for responses, and discuss how appropriate it is to be with a friend in need, sometimes just to sit in silence.

JOB: God and Suffering

3. Prepare these assignments for individuals and small groups. (Download at www.baptistwaypress.org.)

Individual assignment: Draw a picture depicting the emotions of Job and his three friends.

Individual assignment: Write a poem expressing the emotions of Job and his friends.

Individual assignment: Write a newspaper-type story describing Job's situation.

Group 1: Read Job 3:1–10. Select a symbol that expresses Job's emotions in this passage. Cut the symbol using a piece of construction paper, or use other art supplies provided. Prepare to share your ideas with the large group.

Group 2: Read Job 3:11–19. Select a symbol that expresses Job's emotions in this passage. Cut the symbol using a piece of construction paper, or use other art supplies provided. Prepare to share your ideas with the large group.

Group 3: Read Job 3:20–26. Select a symbol that expresses Job's emotions in this passage. Cut the symbol using a piece of construction paper or use other art supplies provided. Prepare to share your ideas with the large group.

Provide scissors, construction papers of various colors (including black), chenille sticks (pipe cleaners work well), and clay or play dough. Use the individual assignments only if someone in the class is skilled in drawing or writing. People asked to do individual assignments should be enlisted ahead of time. Allow about ten minutes for group activities. If the class is small, two people can be a group. If the class is large, assign multiple groups of three or four people performing the same tasks. After the assignments have been completed, invite the individuals and groups to share. Be sensitive to time. Especially if multiple group assignments are made, request that reports be brief. Instruct the groups to read the Bible passage as they give their report. Add other thoughts from Job 3 if needed.

Encourage Application

4. Write the following sentence on the markerboard. "When I face a situation that causes me to ask *why*, I _____ _____." Provide paper and pencils as needed, and ask everyone to complete the sentence with one or more suggestions. After a brief period of thought, lead the class to share ideas. Write the suggestions on the board. After several volunteers have responded, encourage the class to evaluate the list.

5. Ask the class to read the short article "Truths from This Passage" in the *Study Guide*. Lead a discussion evaluating these truths in light of today's lesson.

6. If the class has members or prospective members who are going through times of suffering at this time, plan ways for the class to minister to them. Close in prayer for people who are asking *why*.

Teaching Plan—Lecture and Questions

Connect with Life

1. Lead the class to think of some *why* questions people ponder. Give a few examples to get them thinking. (Why does a month last longer than my money? Why is the grass greener on the other side of the fence? Why can't I get a better job?) After several participants share, make the transition into the Bible study by commenting that Job asked *why* in the passage to be studied. Post the outline of the lesson on the focal wall as follows:

> ### The Agony of Why
> The Appearance of the Friends (2:11–13)
> The Sufferer Speaks (3:1–26)

Guide Bible Study

2. Read or enlist a volunteer to read Job 2:11–13 while the class tries to find the name of the shortest man in the Bible (Bildad, the Shuhite!). Present a brief lecture about the three friends, suggesting some of their positive actions. (Consider the following: They met to discuss how best to help. They went with the right motive. They were moved to find a way to share in Job's pain. They mourned because of Job's pain. They sat in silence when there were no words to offer.)

3. In advance ask a good interpretive reader to practice reading Job 3, attempting to capture the emotions Job expressed. Inform the reader to be prepared to read Job 3:1–10; 3:11–19; and 3:20–26. Write the following questions on the markerboard:
   • Why was I born?
   • Why didn't I die young?
   • Why can't I die now?

   Call on the reader to read Job 3:1–9 while members listen for ways Job asked why he was born. Following the reading, allow participants to share their thoughts. List ideas under the heading "Why was I born?" Present other ideas that are not suggested by the class. Follow the same procedure as the reader reads the other two passages.

Encourage Application

4. Lead the class to respond to questions 1 and 3 in the *Study Guide*. Stimulate responses when dealing with question 1 by suggesting categories such as health, family problems, financial situations, natural disasters, and war. When discussing question 3, consider the appropriateness of Christians asking *why* questions of God.

5. Present the items in the small article "Truths from This Passage" in the *Study Guide*. Lead members to evaluate this list and to suggest other truths they discovered in this lesson.

6. Invite the class to respond to questions 4 and 5 in the *Study Guide*.

7. As time permits, allow the class to share the names of members or prospective members they know who are suffering and asking *why* questions. Plan appropriate ways to minister to these people. Close the class by leading a prayer for them and other people who are suffering.

Background
Job 2:11–13; 4:1—11:20

Main Idea
Would-be helpers whose main intent is to defend their ideas about God provide little help to hurting people.

Question to Explore
What happens when would-be helpers are more interested in defending their ideas about God than in helping people?

Teaching Aim
To lead participants to identify the erroneous approaches of the three friends and to develop positive approaches to helping people who suffer

JOB

God and Suffering

Lesson Three

Helpers Who Are No Help

BIBLE COMMENTS

Understanding the Context

Job's impassioned lament revealed the depth of his despondency. His outburst broke a long, shared silence he had experienced for seven days with his friends. How they knew Job and one another is uncertain, but they learned of his plight and came together to console him. They came when it might have been easier to avoid contact with Job. They identified with him in his suffering, as seen in their actions, which were common in rituals of grief—wailing, tearing their robes, and throwing dust on their heads (Job 2:12). Sitting silently with him for seven days, they showed more empathy for Job by their actions than their words would later express. They sought resources in their faith to help Job understand his plight and overcome it. Their speeches represent a commonly held theological perspective, which Job himself seems to have shared, at least in the beginning.

Clearly, the efforts of Job's friends failed. Their dogmatic theological pronouncements expressed little genuine compassion and limited spiritual insight. Job wanted to test the traditional theology he had received in the crux of his present experience. He could not deny the reality of his suffering in order to conform to demands of an inherited theology. Job did not reject all of the traditional teachings of his friends, but he knew that in his case these teachings could not explain adequately what he had endured.

The initial speech of Job prompted immediate responses from his friends. Each of them spoke in turn, and each of their speeches was followed by Job's response. These dialogues are recorded in two full cycles and part of a third (Job 3—31). The speeches of Eliphaz, Bildad, and Zophar reflect their confidence that they knew the mind of God. They believed Job's suffering had to be the result of his sin. His resistance to their words upset them. In standing his ground against his friends, enduring the baffling silence of God, and bearing his continuing suffering, Job revealed the strength of his character and integrity. The words of a fourth friend, Elihu, recorded in chapters 32—37 convey his anger with Job and his displeasure at the inability of the others to answer him effectively.

Interpreting the Scriptures

When Roles Are Reversed (4:1–6)

4:1–2. Eliphaz appeared cautious and polite as he began his response to Job. He came to console his friend, but his words had the opposite effect. Throughout his first speech (4:1—5:27), Eliphaz contended that the inevitable consequences of sin involve suffering and that all humans sin, bringing suffering on themselves. His unfeeling orthodoxy allowed for no exceptions, not even his friend Job who sat before him suffering for reasons Job could not understand.

4:3–5. Eliphaz noted with some irony that the one who sat in need of comfort before him had been known as an effective comforter of others. Job had helped through his words of wisdom and his acts of compassion. He had "instructed many" (4:3). Note the strong words that describe Job's help. He "strengthened," "supported," and "made firm" people whom trouble threatened to bring down. Now the roles were reversed. Undoubtedly, Job had helped others; but his own suffering may have caused him to call into question the worth of his own counsel.

4:6. Eliphaz reminded Job of Job's core convictions. Central to his life was the genuine "fear of God" that resulted in consistency between his profession of faith and his daily life. Would Job in his impatience now turn from these basic pillars of his life? It is difficult to tell whether Eliphaz was offering this reminder as an encouragement to his friend or as a taunt to point out how far his present despair was from his reputation for hope and confidence. Eliphaz's theology forced him to conclude that because Job was suffering, Job was guilty of sin.

A Crucial Question (4:7–9)

4:7. "Who that was innocent ever perished?" Eliphaz assumed the answer to his rhetorical question was *no one*. Based on his understanding and long experience, he was making an absolute statement. Innocent people are abundantly blessed, at least in the end; and the guilty inevitably suffer and are "cut off." Note that this conviction reflects the contrast between the future of the righteous and the wicked expressed in Psalm 1. Eliphaz did not entertain the possibility of any exception to the rule. The question is especially insensitive when you consider that a significant exception was sitting there before him in the person of the suffering Job. Eliphaz contended that he was arguing from the evidence of personal experience. Yet, he was, at best, guilty of being selective in his use of evidence. Eliphaz would consider nothing that threatened his absolute dogma.

Elaphaz's question turns on the word "perished." The primary meaning is *to wither, dry up, or come to ruin*. It may refer to total destruction in death or to becoming useless. Eliphaz may appear to say to Job: *If you are innocent as you say you are, then you have nothing to worry about. You will be vindicated in the end.* Job, however, in his lament said that he loathed his life and desperately wanted to die. He knew himself to be innocent of anything that should have brought him such misery, and he saw death as the only way out. If Eliphaz were attempting to comfort Job with this question, Job's response reveals how utterly he failed.

4:8–9. In the same way, Eliphaz denied evidence that would question his certainty that evildoers inevitably "perished." They "are consumed" by the blast of an angry God. In reality, though, problems for faith come not only when bad things happen to good people, but also when good things happen to bad people. If the traditional theology of Eliphaz were always true, why do the wicked prosper? See Psalm 73 for a testimony of one who struggled with this side of the issue at hand.

In the remainder of his first speech, Eliphaz questioned whether anyone could be truly right before God (Job 4:17–18). He contended that human beings are inevitably responsible for the trouble in the world and must bear its consequences (5:7). Finally, Eliphaz introduced the idea that Job's suffering might be disciplinary and result in his restoration. He urged Job not to "despise the discipline of the Almighty" (5:17).

Although Eliphaz's motives may have been positive, Job did not find comfort in his words. He heard them as words of judgment, not hope. Job did not question much of his friend's theology. He could not understand, though, Eliphaz's unwillingness to take his suffering seriously and consider his words with more openness. Job continued to resist the attempt to force life experience into the fixed categories of a rigid theology, even when they could not provide adequate explanation or helpful guidance.

Answers That Bring No Comfort (8:1–6)

8:1. Bildad, a traditionalist, had little patience with the struggles of Job. His name can be translated as *beloved of the Lord* or *God's darling*. He did not take Job's pleadings with God or with his friends seriously. He refused to believe there was more to be learned about God's ways with humans than was already known. His words to Job reinforced the speech of Eliphaz and were more specific and harsh in their accusation and direct counsel.

8:2–3. Bildad wanted Job to stop talking. To him Job was a windbag spouting words of sound and fury that were empty of meaning. Bildad took offense at Job's questions concerning God and his frustration with God's silence. He could not conceive of anyone's thinking God would "pervert" justice. God could not act in ways that deviated from the way of righteousness, and neither would God bless one who followed a false way. Reacting to the complaints in Job's lament, Bildad was quick to jump to the defense of God. His speech throughout appears to be defensive.

8:4. Conspicuously absent from Bildad's speech are any words of consolation to Job for the deaths of his children and their families. Instead, in defense of God's justice he suggested that these deaths were divine retribution for the sin of the children, words that must have been difficult for Job to hear.

8:5–6. Bildad's counsel made the assumption that Job had not been acting in faith and obedience to God. The narrative characterized Job as one who feared God and turned away from evil. Job's integrity was his hallmark, but Bildad negated everything in the life of Job prior to his outpouring of lament and question. Bildad assumed Job was in a position of having to earn the favor of a resistant or reluctant God. His counsel reflects a theology of works rather than grace.

The conclusion of Bildad's speech reinforced the basis of his counsel to Job. He challenged Job to look to the settled wisdom of tradition for guidance (8:8–10). That tradition clearly taught that the way of the godless will perish. History also revealed that the way of the wicked produced a false sense of hope that would come to disillusionment (8:11–19). Bildad made a final appeal to Job on the basis of the possibility that he could yet experience restoration and joy.

A Caustic Rebuke (11:1–6,13–15)

11:1. The speeches of Job's friends moved steadily from a tone of controlled civility to one of caustic attack. Zophar, the final speaker in the first cycle of speeches, was evidently the youngest and most certainly the brashest of the three. Although he reflected the same theological position as the others, he spoke with an attitude of arrogance and focused on personal attack.

11:2–4. This speech, like the others, began with a negative reference to the profusion of Job's words of protest and pain. Zophar, however, went beyond regarding them as empty. He began to ridicule Job himself, accusing him of babbling without meaning and mocking God without shame. Zophar was offended especially by Job's claim of innocence and his insistence he was clean in the sight of God. Job was confused and hurt by God's silence as he hoped God would vindicate him.

11:5–6. Zophar rebuked Job for expecting God would speak to him. He claimed that Job was presumptuous in thinking God would answer and that he could even understand the divine wisdom if God did. Zophar wished God would set Job straight. In the absence of God's answer, however, Zophar assumed the role of God's spokesman. Pointedly, Zophar asserted that God had brought less suffering on Job than he really deserved.

Zophar continued his verbal assault on Job's ability to understand the nature of God and God's ways with humans (11:7–12). In a final attack on Job's intelligence, Zophar referred to Job as a "stupid person" who would not be able to understand the ways of God until "a wild ass is born human."

Finally, Zophar held out the promise that if Job repented he might find relief from his suffering, restoration of his reputation, and the renewal of his hope. Zophar warned Job that not to repent, however, would mean he would be trapped in misery with no hope for escape but death.

Focusing on the Meaning

Job's friends may have thought they had done well in their defense of God and their instruction of their friend in the meaning of his suffering. As comforters, however, they failed miserably. Their efforts provide a useful case study in our attempt to learn how to be helpful to those who experience the hard times of life that defy understanding and test faith.

In the time of suffering we should not underestimate the power of presence. When pain is overwhelming and questions loom larger than answers, the touch of a hand, the sharing of tears, and the offering of wordless acts of caring can speak louder than words. Job thought that the silent companionship of his friends at the outset of their visit was the best part of their attempts to help (13:5, 13).

In our desire to help others in crisis, we should develop the art of listening that goes beyond merely understanding the words of another to sensing the hurt of the heart. Each of Job's friends noted that he had spoken at length, and they characterized his words as empty or meaningless, mere "wind" (see 8:1). Yet, none of them demonstrated he had really heard Job's anguish or understood his struggle.

As people who desire to help, we need to remember that one cannot at the same time bring comfort and sit in judgment. Job did not always disagree with the words of his friends, but he reacted strongly to their judgmental attitude. They appear to have concluded already that Job was in the wrong, and they were determined to set him straight for his own good. Hard words can be heard only after one is convinced they come from a loving heart.

A person who helps refrains from offering simplistic answers for complex problems. Often in the face of tragedy or loss we are tempted to fall back on clichés or bromides in order to say something, when there seems to be nothing to say. The easy answer, even though it may contain truth, is difficult to hear when one is struggling with overwhelming issues of suffering and loss.

The most effective helpers allow new experience to deepen their understanding and expand their theology. Such people are always asking, *What can I learn from this? How does this fit with my previous understanding?* They resist forcing personal experiences into stereotypes, and they search for new light from God's word to meet present needs.

TEACHING PLANS

Teaching Plan—Varied Learning Activities

Connect with Life

1. Select one or two of the following case studies that best relate to your class. Change the case study to fit your class better, if needed. Read or describe the situation, and encourage the class to respond to the question. After responses have been discussed, make the transition into the Bible study by indicating that this lesson gives some negative examples of three friends who tried to be helpful.

    Case Study 1: The newspaper reported the arrest of a nineteen-year-old girl for drug use. One of your close friends at work has a daughter with the same name and age. Your friend has not mentioned this situation to you even though there have been ample opportunities. *What response from you would be most helpful?*

    Case Study 2: Franco lost his job two months ago. He has been looking for work but has found nothing. Although Maria, his wife, brings home enough income to keep them from starving, other bills obviously are stacking up. You know Maria and Franco are too proud to ask anyone for financial help, but you would like to help them. *How is the best way?*

    Case Study 3: Four months ago Joe's wife, Sadie, died after a long illness. A lot of their friends attended the funeral, but you are aware that Joe has not had much company since her death. Although you were Sadie's friend and you have been a widow for several years, you aren't sure Joe would appreciate a visit from you. *What could you do to help?*

Case Study 4: Tammy has been diagnosed with cancer. Doctors have told her the situation is grim, and she and Greg are devastated. Word of Tammy's condition circulated fast in your small town. Greg and Tammy have decided to go to a large hospital in another city to get a second opinion. You know Tammy and Greg but do not consider yourself a close friend. *What should you do to help?*

Guide Bible Study

2. Ask participants to examine the content of lessons three and four in their *Study Guides.* Help the class understand that from Job 3 though Job 31 several speeches are delivered by Eliphaz, Bildad, and Zophar with responses from Job. Because the speeches are long and somewhat repetitious, lesson three will consider some of the thoughts of the three friends. Lesson four will deal with Job's responses found in Job 16 and 19. Suggest that the parts of the book not studied in class could be read and studied between sessions.

3. Enlist three effective readers or actors to present the monologues that follow (download at www.baptistwaypress.org). After the speech by Eliphaz, call on a volunteer to read Job 3:1–9. Lead the class to examine the words of Eliphaz and suggest why his words would not be comforting. Follow the same procedure after Bildad and Zophar present their monologues.

Monologue by Eliphaz

Hello! My name is Eliphaz, which means *my God is gold.* My hometown is Teman, which is located in Edom. As you know, my friends Bildad and Zophar and I heard about the suffering of our friend Job. We went to visit him to see whether we could help. Frankly, we were so overwhelmed by Job's condition that we just sat quietly for a long time. Then Job spoke and begged the Lord to let him die.

After Job finished speaking, I decided he needed to hear what I thought about his plight. I reminded Job that throughout his life he had helped a lot of people who were weak and suffering. Now that his fortunes had reversed, he needed to understand that the Lord rewards the righteous and punishes the wicked. After all, no human being can be perfect all of the time. Job should call on the Lord, who will hear and help him.

JOB: God and Suffering

Monologue by Bildad

My name is Bildad, meaning *the Lord loved*. Job just doesn't seem to get it. We know the Lord does not pervert justice. God punishes people who are unrighteous, like Job's children for instance. Do you think the Lord would have killed them if they had been faithful? Of course not. People who get themselves in bad situations like Job is in should repent and seek the Lord. It is the pure and upright who are rewarded. I told Job that if he would just get right with the Lord, he would be restored to his rightful place.

Monologue by Zophar

My name is Zophar. I think Job talks too much. He needs to be quiet and listen to the advice my friends and I are giving him. Job keeps saying he is innocent, but his punishment *must* be the result of sin. I wonder whether Job is receiving all the punishment he deserves. I told Job to stretch out his hands toward the Lord and to put his sins far away. Then and only then will the Lord forgive him and get him out of his misery.

4. Write "True" on the left side of the markerboard and "Not True" on the other side. Ask the class to look in the focal verses to find statements they think are true and statements that are not true. List their responses under the headings. Ask, *What are some statements people say to sufferers today that might not be true or helpful?*

Encourage Application

5. Prepare and distribute the following handout for each participant (download at www.baptistwaypress.org). After the class has completed the activity, lead a discussion based on the responses.

Positive Ways to Help People Who Suffer

Read the list below and make a check mark beside positive ways to help people who suffer. Place an X beside the ways you think are not helpful. Put a question mark beside any statement if you are not sure.

_____ Sit quietly beside the person.

_____ Stay with the person a long time so he or she will not get lonely.

_____ Share your own experience about a similar problem.

_____ Read a comforting passage from the Bible.

_____ Hold hands and lead a prayer.

_____ Leave flowers you picked from your garden.

_____ Provide a meal for the family.

_____ Listen more and speak less.

_____ Explain what you think is happening.

_____ Suggest another doctor that helped a friend.

_____ Offer concrete tasks you could do to help.

_____ Talk about problems in the world.

6. Receive reports from ministry actions accomplish last week as a result of plans made during lesson one. Discuss possibilities for other things to do. Close in prayer for people who are suffering.

Teaching Plan—Lecture and Questions

Connect with Life

1. Refer to the introduction about Hurricane Katrina in the *Study Guide*. Ask, *Why are people quick to suggest that God brings disasters on people because of their sinfulness? What other explanations are there for suffering?*

Guide Bible Study

2. Present a lecture on the format of the Book of Job as the class thumbs through the pages in Job 3—31. Point out that lesson three will deal with some of the ideas presented by the three friends, and lesson four will present some of Job's responses. Refer back to Job 2:11–13 and remind the class about some positive actions of the three friends. Post the outline of the lesson on the focal wall as follows:

> ## Helpers Who Are No Help
> Friends with the Best of Intentions (2:11–13)
> The Trouble with the Friends' Advice (4:1—11:20)

3. Enlist a volunteer to read Job 3:1–9. Using the material in the *Study Guide* and "Bible Comments" in this *Teaching Guide*, present a brief lecture on the content of the speech by Eliphaz. Follow the same procedure to present the thoughts of Bildad and Zophar. After you have presented the three speeches, ask: *What is the common theme of all of the speakers? Why did the friends think what they said would help Job? Why were their speeches not helpful? What statements did the friends make that are not true?*

4. Refer to question 5 in the *Study Guide*. Present a brief lecture comparing the thoughts of Job's friends with Psalm 8 and Psalm 23.

Encourage Application

5. Refer to questions 2 and 3 in the *Study Guide*. List the responses on a markerboard and decide on some good ways to help people who are suffering.

6. Evaluate actions that were accomplished in ministering to people in need as a result of plans made during lesson one. Pray for people who are suffering.

Background

Job 16—17; 19

Main Idea

When human comforters
fail and God seems distant
and even against us, we
can still trust in God.

**Question to
Explore**

What can we do when
it seems we have been
left alone and uncared
for in our suffering?

Teaching Aim

To lead participants to
describe Job's experience
with his friends and with
God and to tell how we
can hope in God even
when we are at our lowest

JOB

God and Suffering

Lesson Four

Longing for Help

BIBLE COMMENTS

Understanding the Context

Genuine dialogue can lead to greater understanding and empathy between people who
have serious disagreement and estrangement.
Too often, however, what begins as construc-
tive dialogue disintegrates into hostile dispute.
People speak but do not wish to listen. They
speak words that will hurt rather than help.
They strive to change the minds of others, but
they will not entertain the possibility of change
for themselves.

The speeches of Job and his three friends in
Job 3—31 demonstrate what can happen when a
quest for understanding and help fails. Each side
accused the other of "windy words" (see Job 16:3)
and long repetitive arguments. Several distinct
themes of these "dialogues" emerge when one
considers all of the speeches and responses.

The speeches reflect Job's growing sense of
isolation and loneliness. Imprisoned by his pain
and loss, Job identified with mortals who "feel
only the pain of their own bodies, and mourn
only for themselves" (14:22). He felt detached
from people and disconnected from God.

Job became increasingly agitated by his
friends. He found their counsel irrelevant and
their charges insensitive. He felt the sting of
their harsh words and untrue accusations. Each

44

side complained of not being understood by the other. Positions hardened, attacks became more negative and personal, and the tone more contentious.

Job's primary contention was with God. He believed God was the ultimate source of his problems but also the only hope for their solution. Job complained he had been closed in or walled off by God. Yet, he repeatedly expressed his "desire to argue my case with God" (13:3). Some of the most passionate passages in Job's responses plead that God "would maintain the right of a mortal with God" (16:21).

In spite of all Job endured, he continued to affirm his innocence before God and his friends. He could not betray what he knew to be true about himself. He refused to believe he would never be vindicated by God. Even in his most miserable moments Job held out a glimmer of hope.

The study passages for this session are from the second cycle of speeches in Job. They contain excerpts of Job's responses to the second speech of Eliphaz and Bildad. They reflect many of these major themes in the total dialogue. Job probed for answers not only to his own problems but also to the deepest questions about human relationships with God.

Interpreting the Scriptures

Miserable Comforters (16:1–5)

16:1–3. Job responded to the second speech of Eliphaz, who had accused him of presumptuous and arrogant speech. Eliphaz had restated his position that suffering comes inevitably to those who are evil and implied that Job was to be identified with them. Job reminded his friends they had come to comfort him, but they had failed to accomplish their mission. Their words were empty and endless and had a negative effect.

16:4–5. In his first speech Eliphaz noted that Job had a reputation as an effective comforter, but now in his suffering Job could not take his own counsel (4:3–5). Job claimed that if their situations were reversed, he could have been a more effective comforter than his friends had been. He knew the words and the gestures that could convey his genuine sympathy for one in grief. The phrase, "shake my head at you," probably refers to a traditional act of sharing grief with another by moving the head from side to side while wailing or moaning.

An Overwhelming Adversary (16:6–8)

Job acknowledged that he was beaten down. He understood that his primary concern was with God, even though Job knew that others were involved in his suffering. As reflected in other speeches, Job knew that he could not stand up to God, who was far greater than he in wisdom, strength, and goodness. He complained that "God has worn me out" and has "shriveled me up." Job no longer had the strength to continue the struggle, and his physical condition was a "witness" against him before the people.

In verses 9–14 Job described his condition in violent and graphic imagery. Note the clause, "God gives me up to the ungodly" (16:11). He sensed that God's hedge of protection no longer surrounded him. Rather, he complained that God had set him up as a target, and God's archers had used him for target practice (16:12–13). Job could no longer feel that he lived in the friendship of God but instead experienced God as his enemy.

Some interpreters see 16:15–17 as a pivot point in Job's experience, reflecting a change in his attitude. He continued to assert integrity in conduct and sincerity in worship. Nevertheless, he put on sackcloth, a symbol of repentance, and bowed to the dust, a rejection of pride. He grieved because of his suffering and searched again to see whether the cause lay within himself.

Hope in Spite of Everything (16:18–21)

16:18. Job pleaded that the earth would "not cover my blood." He feared his cause would perish with him at death and his struggle for justice would soon be forgotten. His words call to mind the story of Cain and Abel. After Cain killed Abel, God said: "Your brother's blood is crying out to me from the ground" (Genesis 4:10). In the Hebrew culture a violent death remained unavenged until the blood was covered by earth (see Ezekiel 24:7). Job did not want his appeal for justice to go in vain but rather to "find no resting place." He did not want it to be filed and forgotten.

16:19. Job could not overcome by himself, and his only hope lay in God's change of heart or the intervention of another. He hoped for help, but he was unclear about the identity of the one who would come to his aid or precisely what could be done. In spite of the enormity of his problem, Job affirmed that he had a "witness . . . in heaven" and asserted that one "that vouches for me is on high." Job needed someone who could verify his story and take the stand as a character witness. In the first cycle of speeches, Job's response to Bildad introduced the idea of the need for help from beyond himself. He complained, "There is no umpire between us" (9:33). He reached out for an arbiter, one who would ensure that the case for each side would be heard fairly. He wanted one who would render justice, and he was confident he would be vindicated.

The Pain of Isolation (19:1–7)

19:1–3. Job expressed disappointment and hurt because of the condemnation he had received from Bildad and his friends. Whoever said, "Sticks and stones may break my bones, but words can never harm me," had evidently never met Job's friends. Job pleaded for an end to the words he said "break me in pieces." Instead of comforting him, the friends repeatedly "cast reproach" and "wrong" him, accusing him without justification.

19:4–5. "My error remains with me." Job contended that any implied sin of his was not a matter to concern others. It was between him and God. Job attacked the motives of his accusers, saying that they had pointed out his sin in order to magnify their own goodness.

19:6–7. As in previous chapters (see Job 9; 13; 17), Job again placed the responsibility for his suffering and hopelessness on God. Job had become isolated from both God and other human beings. He compared his condition to being enclosed in a net, walled off from where he wanted to be, and having no light on his path to enable him to walk. He described himself as crying out when he was attacked, but neither God nor his friends heard or answered his cry. His situation recalls the all too familiar news accounts of people who have been assaulted with others around who did not respond to their cries for help, often simply claiming they did not want to become involved.

Job again recited a lengthy list of illustrations to describe his condition of isolation and humiliation (see 19:9–22). The primary theme seems to be his agony over the loss of his relationships with others and the honor in which he was once held. In Job's culture, shame and honor were powerful factors controlling one's behavior. Note how often in these verses, as in other speeches, Job referred to things that had stripped him of honor and brought humiliation. He complained that he had become a "byword of the peoples" (17:6), a poster boy of shame.

Affirmation of Faith (19:23–27)

19:23–24. Job was aware that his life was "few of days and full of trouble" (14:1). In his earlier response to Eliphaz, he faced his own mortality: "For when a few years have come, I shall go the way from which I shall not return.... My days are extinct, the grave is ready for me" (16:22—17:1). His speeches often refer to the reality of *sheol*, the realm of the dead, and explore the nature of existence after death.

Job seemed resigned that his vindication would not come before his death. Yet, convinced of his innocence, he longed for the opportunity to plead his case before God. He wanted his witness to be preserved "in a book" and even more permanently "engraved on a rock forever." He believed in the ultimate triumph of justice, and he wanted his testimony to endure until that day.

19:25–27. These verses contain the strongest affirmation of faith in the Book of Job: "I know that my Redeemer lives." Yet, these verses are most difficult to understand. One reason is that the Hebrew text is unclear to scholars at crucial points. Another factor is that Christians inevitably view these words through the lens of belief in the living Christ of the New Testament. How did Job understand this affirmation? Did he anticipate it would be fulfilled in this life or beyond? Who was this "Redeemer" to him? These questions have been answered in varied ways throughout the history of interpretation of the book.

19:25. The idea of the *kinsman redeemer* had a rich meaning in Hebrew history. In times of death and family crisis, one nearest in kin had a responsibility to redeem property that may have been lost and to preserve the unity and posterity of the family. The redeemer (Hebrew, *goel*) referred to a person who acted for someone who could not act for himself or herself. The most dramatic illustration of someone who fulfilled this role in the Bible is found in the story of Ruth. When Ruth's husband died, Ruth's kinsman Boaz cared for Ruth and took her as his wife according to the custom of levirate marriage. The term grew in meaning and came to be applied to anyone who went to the aid of another who was oppressed or weak. In time it came to refer to God as the Redeemer of Israel (see Isaiah 41:14; 43:1; Psalm 74:2).

19:26–27. "I shall see God." Job was convinced that in the end he would see God, not as a stranger, but as one he knows is "on my side." In spite of all that had happened, Job believed that God was for him.

Some understand this passage to mean that Job anticipated seeing the Redeemer in this life. More likely, it seems, Job was looking toward a life beyond in which he would continue to exist and see God face to face. Job did not have the understanding of eternity and the life beyond that would come with the gospel. His wrestling with the most basic questions of life in the throes of his suffering, however, brought him to expect something different from the shadowy realm of the dead in *sheol*.

Focusing on the Meaning

Job's experience makes us aware of the need of people for help in times of suffering. At times people's cries for help are not as explicit as those of Job. A person may do something destructive, even self-destructive, in order to get attention. A person may attempt to express need for someone to care but be unable to communicate that need in ways that can gain a response. One of the challenges of Christian living is that of becoming more sensitive to the audible and inaudible cries for help from people all around us who are hurting.

Job reached out for a mediator or advocate. Mediators play essential roles in contemporary life. Whether in international crises, labor-management disputes, marital conflicts, or in many other areas, the "umpire between us" (9:33) is often necessary to bring reconciliation and justice. What is true in human relationships is also true in our dealings with God. We need an arbiter or advocate—one who has the ability to bring us together. When we have experienced God in grace, we have the need to become people who help others find the way.

What Job pleaded for in desperation and affirmed in hope, the gospel proclaims as glorious fact. God has provided the Redeemer to speak in words we can understand and act to do for us what we cannot do for ourselves. The umpire, or witness, or redeemer Job needed and reached for has a name—Jesus Christ.

The New Testament word in response to Job's search is found in Jesus' statement: "I am the way, and the truth, and the life. No one comes to the Father except through me" (John 14:6). Paul affirmed the same truth, which forms the heart of the Christian gospel: "For there is one God; there is also one mediator between God and humankind, Christ Jesus, himself human, who gave himself a ransom for all" (1 Timothy 2:5–6).

TEACHING PLANS

Teaching Plan—Varied Learning Activities

Connect with Life

1. Before class write the following on a markerboard or large sheet of paper:

Bottom Ten

(1) Losing your job or source of income
(2) Having a son or daughter arrested for a felony
(3) Being at the point of death
(4) Being in an automobile accident that leaves you paralyzed
(5) Losing your spouse by death
(6) Experiencing a stock market crash
(7) Getting a bad report about your cancer
(8) Hearing your son or daughter was killed in a drive-by shooting
(9) Losing all of your belongings in a fire
(10) Learning that your spouse is having an affair with your best friend

   Hand every class member a small piece of paper, and ask everyone to select the worst situation on the list by placing a number on the paper. Collect the papers and tally the results to determine which situation received the most votes. Allow class members to add other situations they believe to be a time when they would feel lower than the one receiving the most votes. After dialogue, ask the class to read and consider the suggested study aim.

Guide Bible Study

2. Ask the class to glance at Job 6—7; 9—10; and 12—14 to locate three of Job's responses to Eliphaz, Bildad, and Zophar. Point out that this lesson deals with Job's responses in Job 16; 17; and 19, with the focal passages from chapters 16 and 19.

JOB: God and Suffering

3. Prepare the following Question and Answer Guide, and distribute a copy to each participant (download at www.baptistwaypress.org). Lead the class to read the passages from Job 16 and 19, search the Scriptures for answers, and discuss the answers to the questions. Encourage everyone to use the Question and Answer Guide for making notes.

Question and Answer Guide

Job 16:1–6

(1) What are some words Job used and thoughts he revealed concerning the counsel he had received from his friends?
(2) Paraphrase verses 4–6, capturing Job's thoughts in plain talk.

Job 16:7–8

(3) What faulty theology is expressed in these verses? Why is Job's theology faulty?

Job 16:18–21

(4) What glimmer of hope does Job reveal in this passage?
(5) What concern did Job have?

Job 19:1–7

(6) What words and ideas did Job share about his friends?
(7) What frustration did Job express about God?

Job 19:23–27

(8) Why did Job want his story to be told?
(9) On what Old Testament practice was Job's hope based? (Read and discuss the short article titled "Redeemer.")

Encourage Application

4. On the reverse side of the Question and Answer Guide, print the following questions (download at www.baptistwaypress.org).

How to Hope in God When We Are at Our Lowest

(1) What are some ways Job expressed hope in God even when he was down?

(2) What does Job's experience teach us about hoping in God?

(3) Why can Christians hope in God even more than Job could?

(4) What personal experience could you share telling how God helped you?

Encourage the class to spend a few minutes completing the questions individually or in groups of two or three. Invite volunteers to share their responses. Close with prayer for people who are having difficult experiences.

Teaching Plan—Lecture and Questions

Connect with Life

1. On the markerboard write "Worst-Case Scenario." Ask the class to suggest life situations that would cause people to feel they were at their lowest point. List the responses on the board. Point out that Job probably was feeling at his lowest point in the passages to be studied in this lesson. Briefly review the speeches in Job 3—15, indicating that Job had already responded to Eliphaz, Bildad, and Zophar (one speech to each). Job 16; 17; and 19 present Job's fourth and fifth speeches. Lead the class to examine the Question to Explore and the Study Aim as suggested in the *Study Guide*. Post the outline of the lesson on the focal wall as follows:

Longing for Help
When There Seems to Be No Help (16:1–8, 18–21)
A Repetition of His Sorrow (19:1–7)
The Hope of a Redeemer (19:23–27)

Guide Bible Study

2. Enlist a volunteer to read Job 16:1–8. Present a brief lecture describing how Job felt about the accusations and advice from his friends. Explore the false theology that Job expressed in 16:7–8. Refer to and ask question 1 in the *Study Guide*.

JOB: God and Suffering

3. Encourage the class to listen for Job's glimmer of hope as a volunteer reads 16:18–21. After the reading, allow participants to share what they think Job was hoping. Clarify this passage using the comments in the *Study Guide* and "Bible Comments" in this *Teaching Guide*.

4. Read and summarize Job 19:1–7, pointing out Job's utter frustration with the advice his friends had given and that he received no answer when he called out to God. Ask, *Why might God not answer our prayers immediately?*

5. Enlist a volunteer to read Job 19:23–27. Using Job 19:23–24, lecture briefly on Job's desire that his story be written down so other people could learn from his experience. Suggest that everyone has had experiences that need to be passed on to future generations. Refer to the short article titled "Redeemer" in the *Study Guide*, and present a brief lecture on Job's hope of a redeemer based on his probable understanding. Ask, *What is a Christian view of "redeemer"?*

Encourage Application

6. Lead the class to look at the section in the *Study Guide* titled "Applying This Lesson." Ask members to underline and consider significant ideas in paragraphs 3, 4, 5, and 6. Encourage participants to share responses to questions 3 and 4 in the *Study Guide*.

7. Refer to the short article in the *Study Guide* titled "Helping Those Who Long for Help." Ask class members to decide on ways they could be involved in helping people who are at their lowest point. Close with a prayer for people in need.

Focal Text

Job 38:1–21; 40:1–2

Background

Job 38:1—40:2

Main Idea

Human beings are in
a poor position for
insisting that God live
up to their ideas about
how God should act.

Question to
Explore

In light of our limited
knowledge and
abilities, how should
we relate to God?

Teaching Aim

To lead participants to
summarize God's message
about his superiority and
identify implications
for how we are to see
ourselves and to live

JOB

God and Suffering

Lesson Five

Who Do You Think You Are, Anyway?

BIBLE COMMENTS

Understanding the Context

When people pray in times of trouble, they most often petition God to change things or explain them. Throughout Job's long struggle with suffering, he sought relief from it or understanding of it. Excruciating pain and unending trouble had shaken his most settled certainties. He claimed the right to plead his case before God and repeatedly called on God to answer him. When God finally answered Job out of the whirlwind, the response was not what he expected or had thought he needed.

The final two lessons in the study of Job focus on God's long-awaited response to Job's defense of his innocence and his plea for divine justice. The long cycles of speeches between Job and his friends had ended in stalemate. The often heated exchanges of opinions had brought neither comfort nor understanding. The response of God would seem to have followed naturally after the conclusion of Job's final defense of himself (Job 31:40).

At this point, however, the story took a surprising turn. Elihu, who was not mentioned previously, demanded to be heard. Present during the dialogue, he had grown increasingly upset

54

by what he heard. Described as an angry young man, Elihu claimed to be filled with the Spirit and was obviously full of himself (see 32:1–10). He was angry with Job because of the presumptuous way Job spoke to God. He was also angry with the three friends because they were inept in answering Job.

Elihu's primary purpose was to refute the claims Job had made throughout his experience of suffering and also to come to the defense of God's actions (see Job 32—37). Job had contended he was innocent of sin and complained that God was unjust in bringing suffering on him. He further complained that God would not answer him but continued to remain silent. Elihu responded to Job's contention by saying that God had spoken in various ways, but Job had not been able to comprehend. God had revealed himself in dreams, through Job's suffering, and by interpreters or angel-mediators (see 33:14–28).

Elihu refuted Job's claim of innocence by citing God's knowledge of everything about him including his unknown or unacknowledged sin. Elihu recoiled at Job's charge of God's injustice, contending that God does not punish without cause or treat anyone unjustly. Elihu's sweeping defense of God included impressive descriptions of God's great power in creation, his omniscience, and his justice to all humankind.

The extensive speeches of Elihu in Job 32—37 provide a vigorous defense of God's actions and prepare for the response of God to Job that was yet to come. Although Elihu spoke brashly and displayed an extravagant view of his wisdom, he provided some helpful insight. His final speech challenged Job to listen to God and alluded "to the thunder of his voice" and the rumbling and lightning that accompany God's word (37:2–5). These images provided an appropriate transition to what was to ensue, as God spoke out of the whirlwind.

Interpreting the Scriptures

Out of the Whirlwind (38:1–3)

38:1. "The LORD answered." The name for God used here is Yahweh, the covenant God of Israel. In all the previous speeches other names for God were used, with one exception (12:9). The long silence of Yahweh was broken, and Job finally realized his hope for a direct encounter with God. Yahweh spoke in a theophany, which is a personal or physical appearance or manifestation of God. The voice of God came to Job "out of the whirl-wind." Most often biblical theophanies were experienced as hearing the divine voice and were accompanied by unusual natural phenomena, such as the storm or tempest referred to here.

38:2. Yahweh charged Job with misrepresenting his purpose and plan by his lack of understanding. The New English Bible translates the verse: "Who is this whose ignorant words cloud my design in darkness."[1] Job's limited understanding had led him to make false accusations against God.

38:3. Job had posed questions to God throughout the experience of his suffering and expressed the desire to have opportunity to make his case directly before God. His long-awaited encounter had come, but the questions would not come from Job. God had questions to ask also, and Job would have to be at his best. "Gird up your loins" refers to the practice of tightening one's loose clothing so that it would not be an impediment in a stringent athletic contest or hard physical labor.

God's Creation of the Earth (38:4–7)

God began by asking Job a series of questions about the creation of the earth that Job obviously could not answer in ways that would strengthen his case. Through these questions God enlarged the scope of Job's world from the confining enclosure of his own suffering to the dimensions of all creation. The wisdom and power required to create the earth were clearly beyond those of any human being.

38:4–6. "Where were you. . . ?" The question forced Job to face the brevity of his life in comparison to the eternity of God. He was obviously not present at creation, and neither could he have brought the world into existence or shaped its course. The imagery of God's having "laid the foundation of the earth" invites one to think of the work of creation as that of a builder who carefully builds a large building. Would Job have known the specifications or have been able to lay out the lines of its foundation and walls? "Surely you know!" Throughout the response of God, there is a thread of irony as God turned Job's words back on him and taunted him for his previous self-confidence.

38:7. Job could not claim to have been present at either the design or the completion of creation. He was not there for the laying of the cornerstone. God depicted the celebration of the finished creation as featuring the music of the starry heavens and the accompanying joyful shouts of the angels. The imagery appears intended to stretch the mind of Job and make him aware of the overwhelming greatness of God in relation to himself.

God's Control of the Sea (38:8–11)

Israel was a *sea-fearing* rather than a *sea-faring* people. To them the sea represented powerful and uncontrollable force. It was often the place of death and destruction, a place of uncertain destiny for those who ventured on it. In the Gospels one of the most impressive acts of Jesus was his calming the storm on the Sea of Galilee. The response of the disciples was incredulity (Mark 4:41): "Who then is this, that even the wind and the sea obey him?" In ancient mythology the sea was a symbol of evil and the habitat of monsters of the deep.

38:8–9. God declared to Job his sovereignty over the sea. Neither Job nor any human being could have created and controlled the sea. In an analogy that is difficult to understand fully, God compared the creation of the sea to the birth process and its aftermath. The sea came into being like an infant who "burst out from the womb." Like a mother places swaddling clothes around her newborn child, God covered the sea with "clouds" and "thick darkness."

38:10–11. The primary emphasis is on God's control rather than on the creation of the sea. Note the images of doors that "shut in the sea" (Job 38:8). God declared that he "prescribed bounds for it, and set bars and doors." God spoke to the sea, declaring limits for it: "Here shall your proud waves be stopped." The reality of God's controlling power was implied in the rhetorical questions with which God confronted Job.

God's Preservation of the Universe (38:12–21)

God continued to awe Job by a lengthy recitation of the daily duties of deity. The Hebrew people had no concept of a universe running by itself or according to some impersonal natural law. For them every event in creation was dependent on the presence and power of the Creator. Here in beautiful poetic imagery God affirmed his responsibility for the order of the universe and the dependability of common phenomena too easily taken for granted.

38:12–15. God controls the breaking of each new day. God asked Job ironically whether he were the one who "commanded the morning," even during the short number of days of his life. God set the timetable for the coming of the dawn. Note the beautiful description of dawn's removing the cover of darkness from the earth, like a woman lifting and shaking a skirt. As darkness is removed each morning, the dawn shakes out all kinds of wickedness that thrive under the cover of darkness. The dawn changes the way we see the earth and experience its colors. In contrast, the wicked are those who prefer the darkness, that is, it is light to them. In the true light, they are deprived of their preferred environment in which they find protection.

38:16–18. God alone knows "the expanse of the earth." God alone has access to all the vast regions of the creation. Job had not been to the depths of the sea. He had not explored the sources of the waters of the ocean. He had not been to "the gates of death" and "of deep darkness."

38:19–20. The mystery of the origin of light and darkness was unknown to Job. Here God almost personified them, seeing each as having its separate "dwelling." God alone knows the place where they stay when they are not "on the job." He depicted each as having an assigned territory for its daily work.

38:21. This section concludes with a strong statement of irony. God knew, and by this time Job knew as well, that being God involved far more than Job had ever considered.

The remaining verses of God's first response (38:22—39:30) include continuing questions to Job that probed his knowledge of the mysteries of creation and the management of the world. They set in sharp contrast the power of the Creator God and the limitations of Job. God asked Job: *Can you control the weather? Can you maintain the stars in their courses?* God then turned to the ways of the animal kingdom, especially wild animals not controlled by humans. These questions concerned the lion, mountain goats, deer, wild ass, wild ox, ostrich, horse, hawk, and eagle. The questions reveal details about the unique ways of each of the species. The questions in themselves continued to intimidate Job.

JOB: God and Suffering

A Final Challenge (40:1–2)

The questioning of Job ended, except for one final challenge. God asked Job whether he had enough. Was he ready to give up or did he want to continue to raise questions and respond to God's? The New English Bible translates verse 2: "Is it for a man who disputes with the Almighty to be stubborn? Should he that argues with God answer back?" Now it was Job's turn to keep silent.

Focusing on the Meaning

God's response to Job is surprising for what God did not say as well as for what he did. God did not say that Job's sin had caused his suffering. Also, God did not give Job any explanation at all for his suffering. God did not confirm the charges of Job's friends against him. But neither did he answer the questions Job had raised. What, then, was the value of Job's encounter with God, and what does it imply about our own experience in prayer?

The fundamental question to ask concerning the usefulness of prayer is not *Did I get what I wanted from it?* but rather *What did I become by it?* The issue is not whether I convinced God of my point of view but rather whether I gained God's perspective. In prayer we can experience a kind of Copernican revolution of the soul. We can cease thinking of God as revolving around us and think of God as the center of life around whom we revolve.

Suffering can cause us to raise legitimate questions we want to ask God. It can also, though, blind us to questions we need to ask ourselves. Suffering can shrink our world to the dimensions of our own pain, making it impossible to think of others or to consider the big picture of life. Even more serious, we may neglect to ask ourselves what God is teaching us through this suffering or how it can be used in redemptive ways. In prayer we can open ourselves to God's probing questions as well as experience the freedom to ask God the questions in our own hearts.

Have you ever felt someone had wronged you and found yourself unable to put the matter behind you and move on? Have you built your case against the other person and thought of what you would say if you got the opportunity to meet face to face? Perhaps you have even written a letter that seemed almost to compose itself in the heat of the moment. All of the evidence seemed to provide conclusive proof of your side of the issue. Then, at some point, you met with the other party. You heard another side of the issue and began reluctantly to let yourself consider the matter in a different way. Your strong case began to seem inappropriate. In time reconciliation was possible because of a change in your perspective and attitude.

In prayer we can experience something similar in our relationship with God. Like Job, we can change. Prayer can become less a matter of demanding things of God and more the act of looking at ourselves in the light of God. The mystery and pain of life may remain, but the reality of a relationship with a just and gracious God can make them both endurable and meaningful.

TEACHING PLANS

Teaching Plan—Varied Learning Activities

Connect with Life

1. Write on the markerboard, "Ways People Hear from God." Lead the class to suggest ways people in the Bible heard from God and ways we hear from God today. List the responses under the heading. Make a transition into the Bible study by saying that God answered Job out of a whirlwind. Ask the class to study the small article titled "Theophany" in the *Study Guide*.

Guide Bible Study

2. Introduce Elihu by asking the class to thumb through Job 32:1—37:24. Briefly summarize Elihu's speech using the material in the *Study Guide* and "Understanding the Context" in this *Teaching Guide*. Read or enlist a volunteer to read Job 38:1–3. Point out that God's answer to Job was in the form of questions rather than direct affirmations. Ask, *Why do you think God didn't give Job a direct explanation regarding his situation?*

Job: God and Suffering

3. Bring to class some plain paper, construction paper of varied colors, markers, and pencils. Distribute the following assignments (download at www.baptistwaypress.org) to class members, who will work in groups of two to six people. In small classes, individuals could be given an assignment if you know the person will be able to accomplish it.

Assignment 1. Study Job 38:4–7. Express the meaning of this passage by drawing a picture, writing lyrics to the tune of "Row, Row, Row Your Boat," tearing construction paper to make a symbol, or writing a summary statement in two or three sentences.

Assignment 2. Study Job 38:8–11. Express the meaning of this passage by drawing a picture, writing lyrics to the tune of "Mary Had a Little Lamb," tearing construction paper to make a symbol, or writing a summary statement in two or three sentences.

Assignment 3. Study Job 38:12–15. Express the meaning of this passage by drawing a picture, writing lyrics to the tune of "London Bridge Is Falling Down," tearing construction paper to make a symbol, or writing a summary statement in two or three sentences.

Assignment 4. Study Job 38:16–18. Express the meaning of this passage by drawing a picture, writing lyrics to the tune of "Three Blind Mice," tearing construction paper to make a symbol, or writing a summary statement in two or three sentences.

Assignment 5. Study Job 38:19–21. Express the meaning of this passage by drawing a picture, writing lyrics to the tune of "My Bonnie Lies Over the Ocean," tearing construction paper to make a symbol, or writing a summary statement in two or three sentences.

Allow groups or individuals eight to ten minutes to complete the assignment. Ask them to report. Lyrics to songs could be written on paper so the entire class could sing the words. After each report, read the passage and spend time discussing the content and responding to the questions God asked.

4. Read Job 30:1–2. Ask the class to respond to the question, "Shall a faultfinder contend with the Almighty?" Guide the class to underline the third paragraph (beginning with "How simplistic are our religious and political answers . . . ") under the subtitle "God's Direct

Challenge" in the *Study Guide.* Inquire, *What are some examples of these complex issues or theological insights and ethical interpretations?*

Encourage Application

5. Lead the class to consider the implications of Job's experiences for people today. Write on the left side of the markerboard the word "Mystery" and on the right side the word "Majesty." Ask the class to think of some things we do not know or understand about God and write the responses under "Mystery." Under "Majesty," list things the class suggests that amaze people about God. Lead the class to consider the Question to Explore in the *Study Guide,* "In light of our limited knowledge and abilities, how should we relate to God?"

6. Read the case study in the small article titled, "Discovering God's Grace." Invite the class to suggest insights from Job's encounter with God that might be helpful. Encourage the class members to seek someone who desires God's help and share these concepts with him or her as they seem appropriate. Close with prayer.

Teaching Plan—Lecture and Questions

Connect with Life

1. On the left side of the markerboard write "Wanting Advice from Youth," and on the right side write "Giving Advice to Someone Older." Depending on the age group of the class, ask participants to respond to the headings. For example, if the class members are older, they could list times when they desired or desire advice from youth (for example, on using a computer) and times when they were asked to give advice to someone older than themselves. Younger adults might recall times when an older person asked for advice and how they felt about giving it.

Guide Bible Study

2. Post the lesson outline on the focal wall as follows:

Who Do You Think You Are, Anyway?
The Impatient Words of Youth (32:1—37:24)
At Last God Speaks (38:1–21)
God's Direct Challenge (40:1–2)

Introduce the Bible study by telling the class about Elihu, a young man who decided it was time for him to give advice to Job and his older friends. Read or ask a volunteer to read, Job 32–1–10. Briefly summarize thoughts about Elihu as given in the *Study Guide* and "Understanding the Context" in this *Teaching Guide*.

3. Read Job 38:1–3. Present the information in the small article titled "Theophany" in the *Study Guide*. Ask, *How does God speak to people today?*

4. Enlist a volunteer to read Job 38:4–7. Explain the meaning as needed. Invite one or more participants to respond to this question: *What is the most beautiful scene you have observed about God's creation?*

5. Invite a volunteer to read Job 38:8–11. Explain the meaning as needed. Invite one or more participants who have seen the ocean to answer this question: *How did you feel when you first saw the ocean?*

6. Ask a volunteer to read Job 38:12–15. Explain the meaning as needed. Ask one or more participants to respond to this question: *Where was the most beautiful place you observed a sunrise?*

7. Call on a volunteer to read Job 38:16–18. Explain the meaning as needed. Enlist one or more participants to share the answer to this question: *What is the most amazing thing you have observed about the universe?*

8. Enlist a volunteer to read Job 38:19–21. Explain the meaning as needed. Invite one or more participants to answer this question: *Has growing older affected the way you understand God? How?*

---

9. Read Job 40:1–2. Lecture briefly on the fact that God did not give Job simple answers but instead gave him a challenge to be still and answer God's questions. Review the thoughts given under the heading "God's Direct Challenge" in the *Study Guide*. Ask, *Why doesn't God just tell us what to do and when to do it?*

Encourage Application

10. Lead the class to discuss questions 1, 2, and 4 in the *Study Guide*. Present the two implications given in the *Study Guide* (paragraphs 2 and 4 under the heading "This Lesson and Life"): *There will always be a mystery in our relationship with God, and we must realize the awesome majesty of God.* Lead the class to explore how we should see ourselves and to live in light of God's superiority. Inquire, *What are some other implications that grow out of this study?* Challenge the class to seek people who are struggling with questions about God and share these implications with them. Close with prayer for people who are struggling.

NOTES

1. *The New English Bible* (Oxford University Press and Cambridge University Press, 1970).

Focal Text
Job 40:3–9; 42:1–12a

Background
Job 40:3—42:17

Main Idea
We can have faith and hope that God will provide in spite of our lack of full understanding of why suffering comes.

Question to Explore
What's more important—to know why suffering comes or to know that God will provide for us?

Teaching Aim
To lead participants to suggest implications of Job's response to God and God's provision for Job

JOB

God and Suffering

Faith and Hope When We Don't Understand

BIBLE COMMENTS

Understanding the Context

Job got more than he bargained for in his long-awaited encounter with God. He anticipated God would listen sympathetically as he presented his case and made his appeal for justice. He discovered that God proved to be a tough questioner. God set the agenda and conducted the meeting. God's purpose, however, was not to destroy Job, but to broaden his understanding and revitalize his faith.

God's first extended speech overwhelmed Job (Job 38:1—40:2). He came to a new sense of the vastness of creation and the power and wisdom demanded for its creation and control. In the depth of his suffering, Job had expressed his desire to present his case before God and to demand answers to his complaint. Overwhelmed by the reality of God's power and wisdom, Job responded with a vow of silence. He was chastened but did not yet appear to be fully repentant.

The second divine speech (40:6—41:34) included strong reference to God's commitment to justice as well as his power over creation. In response Job was moved to go beyond silence to full confession of his sin and affirmation of his faith. In neither speech did God accuse Job of moral wrongdoing. Further, God did not give Job an explanation for the cause of his suffering or its purpose. The issues that seemed to be crucial for Job in the beginning came at the end to be less important to him. Through his experience of the reality of God's wisdom, power, and justice, Job was able to live faithfully with the continuing mystery of his suffering.

The focal passages come from both the final section of poetic dialogue and the concluding prose narrative. The final narrative raises a number of difficult questions. The story ends with assurance of God's justice and affirmation of Job's faithfulness. Yet it leaves unanswered the meaning of suffering itself and does not address the reality that many who suffer never in this life experience the restoration of fortune that came to Job. The transition to the conclusion comes abruptly and leaves one reaching for more information. Job's friends, who had been God's staunch defenders, suddenly found themselves on the defensive before God. Job, who had faced God's probing questions, experienced God's confident affirmation. Having sought to plead his own cause before God, Job came to offer prayers in behalf of his friends. Although Job received far more than he had before his suffering, much of his loss, especially his family, was irreplaceable.

Interpreting the Scriptures

A Response of Silence (40:3–5)

40:3. The experience of mystery causes anyone to recognize the inadequacy of human words. In light of Job's often boldly stated desire to present his case before God, his anemic answer to the Almighty may seem surprising. His case, which he once considered to be most convincing, now seemed to be unworthy of restatement.

40:4–5. God's questions brought Job new awareness of the vast scope of the creation and the wonder of God's power and majesty. In awe Job acknowledged he was "of small account." He was *lightweight, insignificant.* A common feature of biblical accounts of direct encounters with God is the immediate sense people have of themselves as inadequate and unworthy. Such experiences inevitably evoked expressions of humility and submission to a greater power and presence.

Job was at a loss for words. He said he would "lay my hand on my mouth" and remain silent. Previously he had insisted that God redress the wrong done to him and the suffering he continued to endure. Job's response conveyed the decision of a reluctant if not fully repentant person who knew himself to have been bested in an uneven contest.

A Renewed Challenge (40:6–9)

40:6–7. Job might have thought his vow of silence would have ended the dialogue with God. The challenge continued, however, implying more rigorous questioning would be forthcoming. God was not satisfied with merely bringing Job to silence; God wanted him to come to repentance for his presumption and to renewal of his commitment.

40:8. God made the second of two specific charges. Job had questioned God's justice. God questioned Job's motive in making his charge. Job believed in his own innocence and was convinced that a just God would reward rather than punish him. Since he suffered with no divine explanation or intervention, Job concluded God was unjust. God implied that Job's motive in accusing God of injustice was to make himself look better in comparison.

40:9. The word "arm" is often used in the Bible as a metaphor meaning *power* or *strength*. The primary usage refers to God's strength in contrast to human power. God asked Job to compare his strength to God's own. God had arrested Job's attention by addressing him with a mighty voice out of the thunderstorm. Could Job do that? God in effect was asking Job to try being God, with all the responsibility for managing the creation and redressing injustice. If Job could do that, God said he would "acknowledge to you that your own right hand can give you victory" (40:14). Job's answers to God's questions would be obvious and embarrassing.

God's first speech had focused on God's power and wisdom in the creation and control of the world. The second speech emphasized God's power in the service of justice (40:10–14). Could Job eradicate injustice? Again, the answer was obvious. God continued to contrast his power with Job's in the extended description of the creation and control of Behemoth and Leviathan. Humans find these beasts, usually identified as the hippopotamus and crocodile, to be wild and uncontrollable. Yet, God manages them easily. Job 41:10–11 poses the rhetorical question: *If Job cannot control these beasts, how can he stand before God as an equal?* These are God's playthings, but they strike fear in humans.

LESSON **6:** Faith and Hope When We Don't Understand

A Confession of Faith (42:1–6)

42:1–2. Job broke his self-imposed silence following God's second speech. His response was different from what he had said after God's first speech, which focused on God's mighty power and wisdom in creation. In that reply Job appeared to be intimidated by God's overwhelming power, and he vowed silence. Here Job acknowledged God's sovereign power and purpose and gave evidence of inner change. Resignation had given way to voluntary and free submission.

42:3. Job cited God's initial question (38:2), which must have been troubling him throughout the encounter. Job confessed that his accusations had gone beyond his understanding, and that he had spoken what he "did not understand." Presuming to be wise, Job in relation to God was out of his league. He spoke of things "too wonderful for me."

42:4–6. Job again cited a challenge given in both of God's speeches (38:3; 40:7). Job's religion had demonstrated a faithful following of tradition even under great stress. Now he characterized his prior relationship with God as one based on hearsay rather than one established by personal experience—"by the hearing of the ear." Job may simply have referred to the long tradition he had inherited and honored. Or, he may have referred more specifically to the many words about God's ways he had endured from his friends who came to visit in his suffering. In either case Job's testimony is a powerful witness to the difference between knowledge *about* God and the personal experience *of* God.

A vision of God in Scripture inevitably turns ones eyes onto oneself. See the experience of Isaiah's vision in the temple (Isaiah 6) as another example. Job's encounter with God led to serious self-examination, resulting in Job's confession: "I despise myself." After God's first speech, Job acknowledged his insignificance. After God's second address, Job confessed his sin. Gone was his presumptuous pride and his distrust of God. Seeing his need to "repent" of his attempt to justify himself, Job looked to the mercy of God as the source of relief. The word used for "repent" is not the more common one that means *to turn back, or return.* Rather, its basic meaning is *to be sorry, or to console oneself.* A common usage is *to find or give comfort or consolation.* Job, who had found no comfort from his friends, found it instead on the ash heap in his confession of his sin to God.

Epilogue: Renewal and Restoration (42:7–12)

The text changes from the form of poetic dialogue to resume a prose narrative, as found in Job 1—2. The friends of Job re-entered the story, and God addressed them. Job had raised serious questions about God's role in his suffering, and he had persisted in arguing them, straining his relationship with God. Yet, God in the end affirmed Job and commended his actions over those of his friends. This is surprising in light of their eagerness to come to the defense of God and champion traditional under-standings of the reasons for evil and suffering.

42:7. God's charge against the friends of Job was they had "not spoken of me what is right." Their defense of God was a mere recital of doctri-naire traditions about God that they offered in a bad spirit toward Job. In contrast, Job had sought to be honest with God and with his friends. Even though Job could be contentious in the dialogues, God commended him for his honesty and his intense desire to have an authentic relation-ship with God.

42:8–9. The epilogue emphasizes the way human relationships affect one's relationship with God. The friends of Job were not only alien-ated from him because of their words, but they also experienced God's wrath. God called them to repent but also to reconcile with Job. They were to offer sacrifices to God, and they were to ask for the prayers of Job to God in their behalf. Job prayed for them, and God "accepted Job's prayer." They experienced God's mercy after the intercession of Job.

42:10–12a. Note also that Job experienced restoration "when he had prayed for his friends." Often it seems impossible to pray for one's ene-mies and even quite difficult to pray for estranged friends. The story seems to imply that Job could not experience the full blessing of God while he was at odds with his friends.

The abundance of Job's material restoration, "twice as much as he had before," is carefully documented in the concluding verses of the narrative. Compare these figures to the description of Job's wealth at the beginning of the story (1:3). Job's restoration also included his relationships to family and friends. He did not receive twice as many children as he had before, but he did have ten children after his loss of his initial family. No mention is made of his wife. Job's restoration was also reflected in the additional one-hundred-and-forty years of life he was granted before his death.

Focusing on the Meaning

The *lived happily ever after* ending of Job is a vindication of Job's faithfulness and integrity in suffering. The outcome seems to verify the counsel Job received earlier from some of his friends that if he endured to the end, he would be rewarded. The story, however, leaves unanswered questions. Not all experiences of unjust or unexplained suffering turn out this way. Many people continue to struggle with whether we can discover meaning in the suffering itself. How can a person remain faithful even in the absence of a happy ending in this life?

Job's total experience points to the conviction that suffering is not so much a problem to be solved intellectually as it is a life journey to be taken faithfully. As the outstanding preacher George A. Buttrick stated: "Life is a journey, not a debate."[1] We do not overcome suffering by explanations of it but by experiences that lead us through it and help us discover meaning in it. Buttrick suggested that Christians travel the road of suffering in a unique way. He described the journey as a way on which the Christian can travel *learning, loving,* and *worshiping.*[2]

In the experience of suffering we can *learn* through pain what we cannot learn in any other way. Suffering can enable us to discover the difference between the passing and the permanent. In stripping away what is superficial and cosmetic, suffering may reveal to us what is truly valuable and enduring. Earlier sections of Job suggest the idea of the disciplinary value of suffering, but this was not the dominant theme.

On the way of suffering we can come to know the importance of *loving and being loved.* Suffering has the power to isolate us from others and turn us inward to our own pain. It can also, however, make us aware of others who care for us and identify with us in our suffering. People who themselves have suffered can become stewards of their own suffering and sorrow in comforting others. The words and actions of these wounded healers provide powerful support and help us strengthen our relationship with God.

On the way of suffering we can travel *worshiping.* Worship for the sufferer may begin, as Job's did, with the desire for answers and divine redress of our grievances. Like Job, we may in time experience the presence of God. Our minds may come to consider a larger world of problems and possibilities. Here we do not find the guarantee that our questions will find their answers so much as a new experience of God's presence that provides enlarged vision of reality. Our questions may come to seem less crucial than before. In worshiping on the way of suffering we come to know a

God who is *for* us and whose love "will not let us go."[3] As a byproduct we may also discover a number of blessings in disguise.

In worship we can discover that although deliverance may not take the form we desire or expect, it nevertheless may bring freedom from the bondage that keeps our lives captive. Like Job in the grip of doubt and uncertainty, we may determine to be honest with God. Like the psalmist in the valley of the deepest darkness, we may experience the shepherding presence that frees from fear. Like others who have encountered evil, we may discover courage we did not think we had. Like people facing death, we may discover hope to overcome not only in this life but for life beyond.

TEACHING PLANS

Teaching Plan—Varied Learning Activities

Connect with Life

1. On the markerboard write, "I once believed _____ was true, but now I think it isn't." Guide the class to discuss in pairs two or three facts, ideas, childhood stories, or other things they previously believed but now do not believe. Allow two or three minutes for discussion and then ask pairs to share their thoughts. Make the transition into the Bible study by saying, *Job evidently changed his mind about his belief about how God relates to human beings.*

Guide Bible Study

2. Enlist a volunteer to read Job 13:3 and 40:3–5 while the class listens for the change in Job's attitude. Point out that Job desired to argue with God about his situation, but when given the opportunity to confront God, Job chose to remain silent. Ask, *What are some reasons Job changed his mind?*

3. Read Job 40:6–9. Point out that God used words like "arm" and "voice" to indicate that Job could not measure up to his Creator. Ask the class to suggest words or sayings that convey the same meaning.

(An example might be a parent who says to a child, "You're getting too big for your britches.")

4. Prior to class enlist a person who enjoys doing research to prepare a two-minute report on the meaning of Behemoth and Leviathan. Summarize Job 40:10—41:34, and then call for the research report.

5. State that in Job 42:1–6, Job affirmed his belief that God alone has the power to direct the ways of God's creation, and there is a divine purpose that no human can either fully understand or thwart. Ask the class to read Job 42:1–6 in unison using the translation in the *Study Guide*. Call attention to Job 42:2, and encourage participants to praise God using other phrases affirming God's goodness and majesty.

6. Read Job 42:7–12a. Refer the class to paragraphs two and three in the *Study Guide* under the heading "The Gift of Something Greater." Allow volunteers to testify about blessings they have received after times of adversity, suffering, or trauma. Lead the class to answer questions 3 and 4 in the *Study Guide*.

Encourage Application

7. Prepare a handout for each participant. On one side of the handout, list the "Implications from This Lesson" and on the reverse side print the "Posttest on Job." (Download both at www.baptistwaypress.org.) Distribute the handout, and ask the class to work individually on the "Implications from This Lesson." Invite volunteers to respond to the questions, and lead a discussion about the implications. Ask, *Can you think of other implications to be considered?* Guide the class to complete the posttest and use it as a review. Allow participants to work together in pairs if they desire. Assure them the test will not be graded. (Answers: 1. a; 2. b; 3. b; 4. c; 5. a; 6. b; 7. c; 8. b.)

Implications from This Lesson

Read the statements below and jot down at least one response to the questions.
   (1) There will always be a gap between human and divine understanding, and so we must learn to trust through faith that God is the good and loving Presence with us through all

of life's struggles. What is something you do not understand about how God deals with humans?

(2) We ought not doubt the sincerity of those who question their suffering or condemn their impatience in seeking answers. Who is an acquaintance who is seeking answers to a life situation? Commit to pray for this person, and ask the class to do so if appropriate.

(3) People who ultimately discover the power of God's loving presence are those who know and acknowledge their need of God. God's grace is sufficient when answers to life's questions elude us. What experiences in your life illustrate this truth?

Posttest on Job

Check the answer you feel is correct according to the Bible.

1. Job is described as a man who
   ____ a. was blameless and upright.
   ____ b. was poor.
   ____ c. was handsome.
2. Satan asked God
   ____ a. Can I kill Job?
   ____ b. Does Job fear God for nothing?
   ____ c. Can I tempt Job to sin?
3. Job's wife
   ____ a. was helpful to Job during his suffering.
   ____ b. gave Job bad advice.
   ____ c. was a mother and wife who grieved over her losses.
4. Eliphaz, Bildad, and Zophar
   ____ a. gave Job wise counsel.
   ____ b. understood how God treats people.
   ____ c. probably had good intentions.
5. Job believed
   ____ a. God caused both good and bad to happen to people.
   ____ b. his wealth and family would be restored.
   ____ c. his friends were faithfully standing by him.
6. Elihu
   ____ a. stayed quiet because he was humble.
   ____ b. thought he had the right answers.
   ____ c. gave good advice to Job.

7. God reminded Job
- ___ a. that Job was a good man.
- ___ b. that people who are blameless will not suffer.
- ___ c. that the Creator is greater than the created.

8. God
- ___ a. always gives back to his faithful followers more than they lost.
- ___ b. will be with his faithful followers during suffering.
- ___ c. promises that people who are faithful will not have any problems.

Teaching Plan—Lecture and Questions

Connect with Life

1. Refer to the introductory remarks in the *Study Guide* giving the writer's feelings when seeing the Grand Canyon for the first time. Invite participants to share times when they had a similar experience. After a few people have shared, make the transition into the Bible study by pointing out that Job must have felt overwhelmed after his encounter with God.

Guide Bible Study

2. Prepare a jot sheet for everyone to use to take notes and to jot down ideas to discuss while listening to brief lectures and responding to questions. Follow the outline on the "Jot Sheet" to present brief lectures on the Bible passages, using comments in the *Study Guide* and "Bible Comments" in this *Teaching Guide*. Discuss responses to the questions. On the reverse side of the same sheet, print the "Posttest on Job" from the other teaching plan to be used later in the session.

Jot Sheet

Take notes as you listen to the brief lectures on the lesson, and jot down responses to the questions.

(1) *Job's Response to God (Job 40:3–5)*. What are some old ideas about God you have had to rethink? Why did Job change his mind about confronting God?

(2) *A Godly Challenge (Job 40:6–9)*. What are some examples of times when people question God's ways?

(3) *The Dialogue Continues (Job 42:1–6)*. What words of praise would you use to express your feelings about God's power and purpose?

(4) *The Gift of Something Greater (Job 42:7–12a)*. Why might the story of Job lead people to conclude that God will bless his faithful followers with wealth? What experiences with God have you had that resulted in surprising discoveries of blessings far different from what you might have expected? Why do you think God directed the three friends to go to Job with sacrifices? Why do you think Job was asked to pray for them?

Encourage Application

3. Direct the class to read the comments in the *Study Guide* under the heading "Applying This Lesson to Life." Ask, *What other implications could be considered?*

4. Lead participants to complete the "Posttest on Job." Allow them to work with a neighbor if preferred. Assure them the test will not be graded. Use the responses to provide a review of the study of Job.

NOTES

1. George A. Buttrick, "The Way of Suffering: Via the Breakthrough," *God, Pain, and Evil* (Nashville: Abingdon, 1966), 152.

2. Buttrick, *God, Pain, and Evil*, 152–167.

3. "O Love That Will Not Let Me Go," words by George Matheson, 1842–1906.

Lesson 6: Faith and Hope When We Don't Understand

Focal Text
Ecclesiastes 1:1–11

Background
Ecclesiastes 1:1–11

Main Idea
Life sometimes seems to have no meaning, with no progress or purpose, going nowhere.

Question to Explore
Do you ever feel that life lacks meaning and is going nowhere?

Teaching Aim
To lead participants to evaluate the Teacher's thought that life seems to be going nowhere and suggest implications for life today

ECCLESIASTES

Struggling to Find Meaning in Life

Life Going Nowhere

BIBLE COMMENTS

Understanding the Context

Studying the Book of Ecclesiastes—what a marvelous opportunity to take a close look at what I discern is one of the more neglected books in Scripture. Across almost fifty years of preaching, I can remember only a couple of sermons preached from this book, and I am not alone.

Although the Book of Ecclesiastes has been neglected in the church, not so in Judaism. The book is read every year in the fall on the fourth day of the Feast of Tabernacles. Some have suggested that this is to add a somber note to what otherwise is a joyful celebration.

Since the Protestant Reformation, theologians have lined up behind one of two opinions about the message and value of Ecclesiastes. (1) Some have said it is a cynical recital of, at best, a lukewarm faith when compared to the higher peaks of Old Testament piety represented in the prophets. (2) Others have said it is an invitation to earthly happiness (see, for example, Ecclesiastes 2:24; 5:19–20).[1]

My take on this book is that it is for the person who finds it hard to believe in the face of the obvious circumstances of life—when, as we might say, *The rules don't fit the game*. Couldn't, for example, a God who is good and all powerful

76

find a way to order things that would rule out hurricanes, tsunamis, and pestilence, and maybe even see that justice is experienced in this life and not just the life to come?

This book is for people who demand the hard answers—answers that do not sugarcoat reality—answers that deal with facts the way they are and not the way we would like them to be. Here is a Teacher who has thought about all of the ambiguities of life in contrast to the neat answers given by conventional piety—work hard, be honest, live moderately. He knows these answers are "a puff of smoke." This is one translation of the Hebrew word *hebel*, also translated "vanity" (KJV, NRSV, NASB) or "meaningless" (NIV). Even though our Teacher calls these answers "a puff of smoke," however, he stubbornly refuses to give up on his faith.

This book is for those who are holding on to their faith and their church by their fingernails. Are they in your Bible study class? You might be surprised to find that they are, but they may well be. Whatever the case, everyone in your class has a family member, a work associate, or a friend who is barely hanging on. Invite your class to join you on this journey. They just might find the very help they need for that friend or family member. Even better, will you and they dare to invite that friend or family member?

Interpreting the Scriptures

Who Is "the Teacher?" (1:1)

The writer identified himself as "the Teacher," translated "the Preacher" in the KJV and NASB. The word translated "Teacher" is *koheleth* in Hebrew. It comes from the verb that means *to assemble* and thus is a title, *teacher of the assembly*.

Ecclesiastes, the English title for the book, comes from the ancient Greek translation of the Old Testament, the Septuagint. In the Septuagint, the title, *Ekklesiastes*, means *a speaker of an assembly*.

The title *koheleth* may have migrated into a proper name much as our English names: *Baker, Carpenter, Smith*. I lived in a small city in East Texas for twenty years. I think most of the people in the town knew me, but less than ten percent could have called me by name. They simply called me "Preacher."

The writer of the book never gives himself a personal name. He calls himself by title and drops hints as to his identity: ". . . son of David, king in Jerusalem" (1:1) and "I, the Teacher, was king over Israel in Jerusalem" (Ecclesiastes 1:12), never saying, *I, Solomon.*

The language of Ecclesiastes is post-exilic Hebrew (500 B.C. to 200 B.C.), not the language of the times of David and Solomon. This fact has led even some conservative Old Testament scholars to conclude that the author was a post-exilic Hebrew scholar who identified himself and his writing with the wisdom literature of the times and image of Solomon, Israel's wisest king.[2] This identification with Solomon probably aided the book's inclusion into the canonical list of Jewish Scriptures at the Council of Jamnia in A.D. 90. The authenticity and authority of the book, however, does not rest on our ability to discern authorship with certainty. In referring to the author, I will simply use the title/name he has given us, "the Teacher."

The Theme of the Book (1:2)

"'Meaningless! Meaningless!' says the Teacher. 'Utterly meaningless! Everything is meaningless'" (Eccles. 1:2).

Hebel is the Hebrew word translated "meaningless" in the NIV and "vanity" in the KJV, NRSV, and NASB. In addition to "meaningless," *hebel* is translated "worthless," "nonsense," "empty," "breath," "fleeting vapor," "useless," "futility," and "dishonest" in the NIV.

The word suggests a lack of substance. You can't grab hold of it. The word also suggests that something doesn't last. It is "here today; gone tomorrow." The word *hebel* brackets the Book of Ecclesiastes (1:2 and 12:8) and points us to the theme.

The Teacher wanted to answer the question, *How can life best be lived?* He had tried all that the pietistic wisdom of the day had instructed, and he pronounced them all to be *hebel*—"a puff of smoke." So, in light of the meaninglessness of life, how ought we to live? The Teacher showed the need for a doctrine of life after death where the scales of justice are placed in balance. As we study, let us remember that Christians have that assurance for which the Teacher longed.

Illustrations Supporting the Theme of the Book (1:3–11)

1:3. "What does man gain from all his labor at which he toils under the sun?" The implied answer is *hebel*—"a puff of smoke," lacking in substance and short-lived. Life requires painful and hard labor, but it does not return a profit. The word translated "gain" is used to express profit accruing from a business transaction, but it need not be limited to financial profit. It may include enjoyment of life and work (3:12–13), control of one's destiny (6:12; 8:7–8), and perhaps the preservation of one's legacy by future generations (2:18–23).

"Labor" refers to all activities by which life is sustained. People may find enjoyment in their labor, and it may sustain life, but it offers no permanent satisfaction.

The midlife crisis is real for many people. It is a time when men and women in their late thirties to early forties realize that they are not going to achieve their goals for life. The crisis is generated as their goals go through a "reality adjustment." This was not, however, the crisis faced by the Teacher. His crisis was the product brought on by the *achievement* of his goals, only to find that achieving these goals did not deliver the meaning for which he had longed. Having achieved it all, he was left asking, *Is this all there is?* The expression " . . . under the sun" means "here on earth" and is so translated in the Contemporary English Version (cev).[3]

Rabbi Harold Kushner, known for his book dealing with the issues of the Book of Job, *When Bad Things Happen to Good People* (1981), had a book published a few years later (1986) dealing with the issues raised by the Teacher: *When All You Ever Wanted Isn't Enough: The Search for a Life That Matters.*

1:4–8. Nature leads to frustration. Science describes physical laws that appear to have always been in place. If asked, though, to speak to some ultimate end or purpose revealed in nature's laws, science can tell us nothing. The biblical view of nature is that it testifies to a Creator but does not compel belief in him (see Psalm 19; Romans 1:20).

The Teacher contended that due to the cyclical nature of creation, meaning and purpose cannot be found there. The logic is that if everything is endlessly cyclical, how can human beings break out of the temporal circle into a state that leads somewhere?

"All things are wearisome" (Eccles. 1:8). All of the things that human beings can observe of the aimless movement of the natural world cause the spirit to become weary at seeing and hearing the endless repetition.

1:9–11. History fails because it is just *same old same old.* As in nature, so in human history, things repeat themselves. It is as Yogi Berra is reported to have said: "It is just *déjà vu* all over again." A comedic rendering of the thought in verses 9–11 is the Bill Murray movie, *Groundhog Day* (1993). In the movie, weather forecaster Phil Connors (Bill Murray) lives out Groundhog Day over and over again in the little town of Punxsutawney, Pennsylvania.

"Is there anything of which one can say, 'Look! This is something new'?" (1:10). The only reason that it appears to be "something new" is that "there is no remembrance of men of old" (1:11). Too, there will continue to be things in the future that will appear to be new because "even those who are yet to come will not be remembered by those who follow" (1:11).

Focusing on the Meaning

Arthur Miller's play *The Death of a Salesman*[4] is an American tragedy. It is the story of Willy Loman, who had the goal of being number one as a salesman. His goal put him in competition with everyone and cut him off from relationships. He tied his self-worth into his dream, and when he failed to be number one as a salesman, his life was empty and mean- ingless. His emptiness led him to take his own life by driving his old car into a tree. Willy could have resonated with the Teacher: "'Meaningless! Meaningless!' says the Teacher. 'Utterly meaningless! Everything is mean- ingless'" (1:2).[5]

The ultimate end of "Meaningless! Meaningless! . . . Everything is meaningless" (1:2) is nihilism. Nihilism is a philosophy that stresses an extreme form of skepticism that denies all existence. It holds that all values are baseless and that nothing can be known.

Dr. J. Budziszewski is professor of Philosophy at the University of Texas at Austin. When Dr. Budziszewski began his teaching career, he was a self-described nihilist. He has published a paper on the internet on how he became a nihilist and how he escaped from nihilism and returned to the Christian teaching of his youth. If you think this might be helpful to you or to someone in your class, do an internet search with the words "Escape from Nihilism," the title of his paper.[6]

The Teacher paved the way for a gospel of abundant life (John 10:10). The Old Covenant anticipates a New Covenant, and this is never more evident than in the Book of Ecclesiastes.

TEACHING PLANS

Teaching Plan—Varied Learning Activities

Connect with Life

1. Invite various class members to comment about any jewelry they are wearing (wedding ring, bracelet that was a gift from a child, cuff links, tie tack, watch, etc.). Comment that for many of us such items are special. They are significant and meaningful. Then distribute candy bracelets, necklaces, or play jewelry to class members. Point out that while this toy jewelry might be special to a child, it has very little meaning, if any, for adult class members. It is not associated with any memory or special occasion; you did not get to choose it; it does not match your clothing; it is cheaply made; and so on.

2. Enlist a class member to read Ecclesiastes 1:1–2, and then ask participants to recite together the thoughts in the latter part of verse 2, "Utterly meaningless! Everything is meaningless." Ask, *Do you think people today feel that way sometimes?* Call for examples. Remind class members that the author of the Book of Ecclesiastes strikes a chord with us because sometimes life can feel more like play jewelry than its real counterpart. Life can seem to have no meaning, with no progress or purpose, going nowhere.

3. Rather than using jewelry, you may want to make use of the basic idea of the jewelry activity by contrasting significant pictures (class members sharing wallet pictures of family and friends, or provide pictures from class activities and outings) to pictures of unknown people from magazine clippings.

Guide Bible Study

4. Enlist someone in advance to summarize briefly information in the *Study Guide* about Ecclesiastes in "Introducing Ecclesiastes: Struggling to Find Meaning in Life" and "An Overview" in the lesson comments. Or, provide this summary yourself.

5. Call attention to Ecclesiastes 1:1–3. Ask, *What do you think the Teacher in Ecclesiastes really wanted? What was he searching for?* After discussion, invite members to formulate a list of questions people often ask that echo the feelings of the Teacher. Questions might include

   • Is there a purpose for my life?
   • Does life really have meaning?
   • How am I supposed to know and understand God's will?
   • Is there nothing more than this?
   • How can life be so disappointing?

6. Comment that for the Teacher, meaningless life was not the result of a life without activity. Use Ecclesiastes 3:1–8 to point out that the author knew about life. He had lived and watched others live; he had experienced all the elements that life had to offer! In contrast, meaningless life is one lived without the power and presence of God.

7. Enlist a volunteer to read 1:4–9 while the class listens for the various images from nature. Ask class members to notice the role of nature's elements as you present a brief overview of these verses using information in the *Study Guide* and "Bible Comments" in this *Teaching Guide.*

8. Call attention to the sentence in verse 8, "There is nothing new under the sun." Point out that all people, in all places, in all times, must face the prospect of life going nowhere, or life being meaningless and without purpose.

9. Separate class members into four small groups (if class size allows), and assign each group one of the following passages:
   • John 3:1–8 (Nicodemus)
   • Matthew 19:16–22 (The Rich Young Man)
   • John 4:7–38 (The Woman at the Well)
   • Mark 2:14–17 (Levi)

   Give groups a few minutes to consider the following questions, and then ask them to share their ideas with the entire class (a copy of these assignments is available for downloading at www.baptistwaypress.org):
   • In what ways did the person in your passage struggle with life going nowhere?

- How might this person relate to the Teacher in Ecclesiastes?
- How did the person try to fill the emptiness of life?
- What difference did Jesus make in the life of this person?

10. Point out that the Bible personalities just studied had at least one thing in common—each person had a hole in his or her heart. It was a longing, a void, an emptiness that only God could fill.

11. Read Ecclesiastes 1:10–11. Note that the Teacher's honest despair was not the end for him; rather, it was the beginning. He was indeed on a journey, a journey from nowhere to somewhere!

Encourage Application

12. Lead class members to respond true or false to the following comments based on Ecclesiastes and then to discuss them.
    - Life lived on the surface draws one into absurdity.
    - There is nothing new under the sun.
    - Trying to change the course of your life is futile.
    - Our existence parallels the cyclical existence of the rest of nature (the earth, sun, wind, rivers, seas, etc.).
    - Searching for meaning in life leads to a dead end.

13. Display a sign (or poster) that says "Dead End." Ask, *How smart is it to travel to the end of the road just to make sure the sign is correct?* Comment that for a person who feels life is at a dead end, perhaps like the Teacher in Ecclesiastes, or perhaps like some of us, it may be most helpful to stop, ask, consider, and question. *What implications do you see for life today in the Teacher's thought that life seems to be going nowhere?*

14. Inquire, *Do you feel like life is like toy jewelry or more like a precious treasure that you value with every breath?* Remind participants that God brings meaning and purpose to our very existence! Close with prayer.

Teaching Plan—Lecture and Questions

Connect with Life

1. Share the following: A man and his wife get into their car, and he drives them to dinner. A few minutes later the wife asks, "Where are we going?" The man responds, "I have no idea, but we are making good time!" Comment that life can sometimes seem to have no meaning, with no progress or purpose, going nowhere.

2. State that today's study moves from the Book of Job to the Book of Ecclesiastes. Use the information in "Introducing Dealing with Hard Times: Job, Ecclesiastes, Habakkuk, Lamentations" and "Introducing Ecclesiastes: Struggling to Find Meaning in Life" in the *Study Guide* to remind class members of the relationship among these books. To give a further overview of the three lessons on Ecclesiastes you may want to scan the entire book and point out familiar verses such as 3:1–10, 14; 4:9–12; 5:10; 11:1; and 12:1. Conclude your overview by calling attention to Ecclesiastes 12:13. Read the verse aloud and comment that life without God indeed goes nowhere.

Guide Bible Study

3. Share the following lesson outline with class members (you may want to display it on a markerboard or poster):

Life Going Nowhere

An Overview (1:1–3)
What Nature Reveals About God and Meaningfulness (1:4–9)
Hope or Despair? (1:10–11)

---

4. Read verses 1–3 aloud to the class while they listen for the theme of the book. Ask, *Where do people search for meaning and fulfillment in life?* (Responses may include job, spouse, children, money, possessions, power, control, entertainment, social clubs, service organizations, and even church.)

---

5. Read verses 4–9 while the class listens for elements of nature that are mentioned. Ask class members to share responses to the following questions:
   - What elements of nature does the Teacher list?
   - What is the significance of these elements?
   - What do you notice about the consistency of the earth, sun, wind, rivers, and seas?
   - According to the Teacher, what does the cycle of nature suggest about life?
   - Can nature bring meaning and purpose to our lives?

6. Call attention to the statement in verse 8, "All things are wearisome." Point out that for the Teacher in Ecclesiastes, and for us, the things we mistakenly use to find fulfillment in life can become the very things that can bring disillusionment and discontentment (see step 4).

7. Lead members to look at another statement in verse 8, "The eye never has enough of seeing, nor the ear its fill of hearing." Ask, *Can our senses bring fulfillment? How and how not?* Allow time for discussion.

8. Read verses 10–11 while the class listens for ideas about life. Note that the *Study Guide* suggests that these words represent grief work. The Teacher in Ecclesiastes, much like Job, Habakkuk, and the writer of Lamentations grieved because life experiences, within themselves, did not bring meaning and contentment to his soul.

Encourage Application

9. Call attention to the study questions in the *Study Guide*. Discuss these questions aloud as time permits.

10. Share this illustration: A few years ago a new thrill ride opened at Six Flags Over Texas Amusement Park in Arlington, Texas. The Titan roller coaster towers 255 feet above the earth, with more than a mile of track. With a top speed of eighty-five miles per hour, the Titan can hurl 1,600 riders per hour through three-and-a-half minutes of drops, spirals, camelback hills, curves, and helixes. But even while the Titan inspires thrill seekers and brings the latest in technology to the roller coaster world, it cannot provide a lasting or meaningful

life experience. The ride is short-lived with no lasting effect. In fact, riders get off at the same place they get on. In spite of the great ride, they have actually gone nowhere!

11. In a moment of silence, encourage class members to examine their lives. Ask them to respond silently to the following reflective questions:
    • Are you living with meaning and purpose?
    • Are you on a journey with God, or merely going up and down and around and around?
    • What do you sense God wanting to do in your life today?
    • How can you live this week to better demonstrate God's presence and power in your life?

    Close with prayer.

NOTES

1. Unless otherwise indicated, all Scripture quotations in lessons 7–9 on Ecclesiastes are from the New International Version.

2. See Edward J. Young, *An Introduction to the Old Testament* (Grand Rapids, Michigan: Eerdmans, 1960), 367–369.

3. American Bible Society, 1995.

4. Arthur Miller, *The Death of a Salesman* (New York: Penguin Books, 1949, 1976).

5. For some great quotes on the problem of meaninglessness, go to www.sermonillustrations.com, click on M, and look for the word "meaninglessness."

6. Or go to www.leaderu.com, and do a search from there.

Focal Text
Ecclesiastes 1:12—
2:17, 22–23

Background
Ecclesiastes 1:12—2:26

Main Idea
Even the noblest efforts of human life are not enough in themselves to bring a deep and lasting sense that life is meaningful and worthwhile.

Question to Explore
What is the sense of it all?

Teaching Aim
To lead participants to state why current human efforts to find the meaning human beings want in life fail

ECCLESIASTES

Struggling to Find Meaning in Life

Lesson Eight

Nothing Works

BIBLE COMMENTS

Understanding the Context

In the first lesson on Ecclesiastes, we discovered the theme of the book: Life is "a puff of smoke." You cannot hold it with your hand, and it is transitory. The Teacher's word was *hebel*, a Hebrew word that is translated "meaningless" in the NIV. "'Meaningless! Meaningless!' says the Teacher. 'Utterly meaningless! Everything is meaningless'" (Ecclesiastes 1:2).

In the Scripture passage for the first lesson on the book, the theme of meaninglessness was illustrated in nature and history. Nature was meaningless because all that a person could observe led to the assessment that the movement of the natural world was endlessly repetitive. All of the things that human beings can observe of the seemingly aimless movement of the natural world cause the spirit to become weary at seeing and hearing the endless repetition. Nature testifies to a Creator, but it does not compel belief in him.

We also had illustrated for us in that lesson that history was meaningless because it was *same old same old*. "Is there anything of which one can say, 'Look! This is something new'? It was here already, long ago; it was here before our time" (Eccles. 1:10).

Today's lesson comprises the remaining verses of chapter 1 and all of chapter 2. The Teacher, in his earlier life, had conducted a grand experiment. He had tried wisdom or learning as an end in itself and had discovered it to be meaningless. He had run after the pleasure goddess and found her wanting as a source of meaning for life. Finally he made some observations about meaning. Some things, while still meaningless, are better than other things. Because death levels everything, though, even the things that are better than others are but "puffs of smoke"— *hebel*—meaningless. "Like the fool, the wise man too must die!" (2:16).

Interpreting the Scriptures

The Teacher Tries Wisdom/Education as a Way to Find Meaning (1:12–18)

1:12. "I, the Teacher, was king over Israel in Jerusalem." The kingly position taken in Ecclesiastes 1:1 is reaffirmed here. Those who believe our Teacher was not Solomon but a wise academic living in the third century B.C. point to this verse for support, saying, *There never was a time when Solomon was previously king over Israel in Jerusalem. He was king until his death and was succeeded by his son Rehoboam.* Along these lines, it is important to consider also verse 16 ("I have grown and increased in wisdom more than anyone who has ruled over Jerusalem before me. . . ."). This is a strange way of speaking if the Teacher was Solomon, who lived in the tenth century B.C. Only one person ruled over Israel in Jerusalem before Solomon, and that was David his father. Similar wording is found also in 2:7, 9.

1:13–16. Verse 13 contains the first mention of God in the Book of Ecclesiastes. The Teacher used the name for God that emphasizes God's power—*Elohiym*, meaning *God Almighty.* This word is also used to identify the God of creation, "In the beginning God [*Elohiym*] created the heavens and the earth" (Genesis 1:1). The Teacher said he "devoted [himself] to study and to explore. . . ." Together the words imply exhaustive study. "To study" means *to delve deeply into a subject matter.* "To explore" points to a broad range of subjects covered.

Three conclusions follow. First, in verse 13, "What a heavy burden God has laid on men!" People have a compulsion to try to figure out the meaning of their lives. Since, however, life is "a puff of smoke," they are doomed to continue to seek the meaning of that which is meaningless.

This situation is reminiscent of the Greek mythological king of Corinth, Sisyphus, who was condemned for all of eternity to roll a huge stone up a hill. Before the rock reached the top it always rolled back down the hill, and he had to begin again. The worst punishment the gods could imagine was to be involved in pointless, unending activities. The Teacher contended that the search for meaning was similar to this.

The second conclusion (Eccles. 1:14) is that people are frustrated because of this situation. They desire gain in life (1:3), satisfaction in the life around them (1:8), and a sense that history is going somewhere (1:9–11). All of these elude them, however. People are frustrated because they have an ambition for that which is unattainable—"a chasing after the wind."

The third conclusion (1:15) is an explanation of why the Teacher was so frustrated. It was because there are twists ("What is twisted") and gaps ("what is lacking") in the thought processes. No matter how thorough the philosopher is in the thinking process, some twists cannot be straightened, and some gaps cannot be filled. Wisdom may help in some things, but it is powerless before the fundamental problem of life—*What is the meaning of it all?*

1:17. "Then I applied myself to the understanding of wisdom, and also of madness and folly. . . ." The introduction of "madness and folly" to the discussion seems arbitrary, but perhaps the point is that as the Teacher thought about wisdom and knowledge, he kept one eye on the alternatives, "madness and folly," anticipating the next section of Scripture.

1:18. Let's bring this proverbial cry into the twenty-first century. Here is a young man whose family values education. The parents finished high school but were denied the opportunity of studying at the university level. They know, however, intuitively that the way to "make it" is through education. They drill this viewpoint into their son's head. He works hard and is valedictorian of his class. He attends a prominent university near his home on a full academic scholarship. After finishing his master's degree, he studies for his Ph.D. at a prestigious university in the East. When he finishes his Ph.D., he is invited to join the faculty of another prestigious university. By now he has a wife and two small children. He find himself having to live forty miles from the university because of the high cost of housing. He finds commuting in the heavy traffic to take up so much time that he puts a cot in his office and stays in the office during the week, leaving him only the weekends with the family. He awakens one day and realizes that his children are teenagers, and he doesn't know them. He might well quote the Teacher: "For with much wisdom comes much sorrow; the more knowledge, the more grief."

The words of Jesus come to mind, "What good will it be for a man if he gains the whole world, yet forfeits his soul?" (Matthew 16:26).

Pleasure and Possessions Fail to Provide Meaning (2:1–11)

2:1–2. Having finished the experiment of making wisdom (education) the stackpole for life with meaning, our Teacher turned to pleasure and possessions. In verses 1–2, the Teacher summarized the experiment and its result. He gave himself to unrestrained pleasures, but these failed him in giving meaning to life. The experiment ended in the conclusion (2:2) that "laughter . . . is foolish," and pleasure accomplishes nothing.

2:3–10. These verses describe in detail the Teacher's experiment with pleasure. The Teacher was not advocating mindless debauchery. You would never have found him staggering in drunkenness or helpless in an addiction. In all that he did he was determined to remain in control ("my mind still guiding me with wisdom," 2:3). He would seek the stimulus of wine but never be its victim.

Adding to wine, the Teacher tried accumulation: houses, vineyards, gardens, parks. To care for these possessions, he built reservoirs (2:6) to irrigate his gardens during Palestine's dry season (May to October each year). He acquired flocks and herds to the extent that he was the envy of all of his contemporaries (2:7b). He bought slaves to work his vineyards, gardens, and parks and tend his livestock (2:7a). He "amassed silver and gold" from neighboring kings and provinces (2:8a). Too, our Teacher was a patron of the arts: "In the cultural arts, I organized men's and women's choirs and orchestras" (2:8b, The Living Bible[1]).

In his experiment of running after pleasure, nothing our Teacher's eye delighted in was out of reach (2:10). This included sexual lusts associated with a harem (2:8c).

If our Teacher were alive today, what would he be like? Perhaps he (or she) would be the CEO of a large international corporation, with villas in Switzerland and in the Bahamas, as well as a penthouse in London and another in New York. Such a person might be "self-made," with every reason to be proud of his or her achievements and the merit badges of success that had been collected. Of course, even a person of lesser wealth and achievement but with similar motivations might well fit the profile.

2:11. And the verdict? That which was previously handed down on wisdom is now applied to pleasure. It was all meaningless. It meant nothing. It was simply *hebel*—only "a puff of smoke." It was not that the Teacher had any regrets. The morality of his project was not under consideration. His experiment simply proved that pursuing pleasure was not the answer to life's ultimate meaning.

Wisdom, While Not Providing Meaning, Is Better Than Folly (2:12–17)

2:12. "What more can the king's successor do than what has already been done?" A paraphrase of this might be: *How will future kings handle this problem I have faced? What kind of person will my successor be in his evaluation of life as to its meaning?*

2:13–14. At this point the doctrine of traditional piety is conceded. Wisdom is of value. The wise person will avoid many of the stumbling blocks that trip up the fool because the wise person sees "while the fool walks in the darkness." The Teacher's previous criticism of wisdom is not of wisdom in every respect, but of wisdom as the highest good, the answer to the question of life's meaning. There is a practical value to wisdom, but there are a couple of "flies in the ointment."

2:15–17. Fly number one: In the long run, whether you are a wise person or a fool, you share the same fate. Both the wise and the fool come face to face with death, and neither will long be remembered.

"Like the fool, the wise man too must die!" (2:16). This statement should be read more as protest than simply as anguish. *It is not fair!* the Teacher might have said. *Why should all of the distinctions that we make in life, like the distinction between a wise person and a fool, mean nothing when we come face to face with the one certainty that comes to all of us?* This thought confirms the earlier verdict—*Meaningless; all of it, meaningless!*

2:18–23. Fly number two: You may use your skills, your abilities, your talents, working hard and long hours to create for yourself a secure future. Then death strikes. Then all that you have worked for so strenuously passes to someone who has not lifted a finger to earn it. The person who receives your estate may not have your abilities or your drive; in fact, your successor may be a fool. This is not a comforting thought.

So, Enjoy (2:24–26)

Living for work, for learning, or for pleasure has ended in a colossal disappointment. It is *hebel*—meaningless!

So, what advice does our Teacher have for his students? After the gloominess of chapters 1—2, here is the first ray of sunshine. Listen up! The best thing you can do in the midst of meaninglessness is to enjoy life—enjoy meaningful relationships with friends and family and find joy in work. It doesn't get any better than that, the Teacher says in these verses! (Stay tuned. The Teacher will have more to say in the next passages of Scripture to be studied.) Note, however, this is joy *in* your work and not joy just *in the results of* your work.

These are the best things in life, *and* they are God's gifts. Elsewhere they are called blessings.

Focusing on the Meaning

There are many wells in life from which to drink. The Teacher had taken great gulps from the wells offered in his day: work, education, and pleasure. He had found them unable to satisfy his thirst for a life with meaning and purpose. Those who live in the time of the New Covenant know something for which the Teacher, writing before the time of Jesus, could only yearn, namely, that *only Jesus can slake our thirst for life with a meaning and purpose.*

To the Samaritan woman at the well, Jesus said: "If you knew the gift of God and who it is that asks you for a drink, you would have asked him and he would have given you living water.... Everyone who drinks this [physical] water will be thirsty again, but whoever drinks the water I give him will never thirst. Indeed, the water I give him will become in him a spring of water welling up to eternal life" (John 4:10, 13–14).

Every day for seven days during the Feast of Tabernacles that celebrated God's protection and provision during the wilderness wandering, a priest filled a golden vessel with water at the pool of Siloam and carried it to the temple. There it was received with the blast of a trumpet and the words of

Isaiah, "With joy you will draw water from the wells of salvation" (Isaiah 12:3). On the eighth day, the last day of the feast, the priest came with an empty vessel, celebrating the entrance into the Promised Land, where the desert provision of water was no longer needed. On that day, Jesus cried out in a loud voice, "If anyone is thirsty, let him come to me and drink. Whoever believes in me, as the Scripture has said, streams of living water will flow from within him" (John 7:37–38).[2]

TEACHING PLANS

Teaching Plan—Varied Learning Activities

Connect with Life

1. Tell class members that you know, without a doubt, that they are the smartest people in the entire church, and today you are going to prove it with a brief quiz! Ask the following trivia questions (feel free to add others of your own):
   * What is the largest city in our state?
   * How many yards are there in a football field? (100 yards, goal line to goal line)
   * What are the first four books of the New Testament called? Name them. (the Gospels, Matthew, Mark, Luke, John)
   * Who was the disciple whom Jesus invited to walk on water? (Peter)
   * Which book of the Bible contains the creation account? (Genesis)
   * Who is known as the wisest man in the Bible? (Solomon)

2. Share this play on words with participants, *You may know all the answers and still not know The Answer.* Ask class members what they think the statement means. Then comment that the Teacher knew all the answers and had all the pleasures life could offer, but he still felt incomplete and insecure. He was a know-it-all whose life was empty and unfulfilled.

Guide Bible Study

3. Call attention to a previously displayed poster with the main idea of today's study, "Even the noblest efforts of human life are nor enough in themselves to bring a deep and lasting sense that life is meaningful and worthwhile." Comment that the overall question that today's study will explore is, "What is the sense of it all?"

4. Write the two focal topics on a markerboard, as follows. Leave space under each heading for class members to fill in the columns as they explore the corresponding biblical passages.

Wisdom's Failure (1:12–18)	Pleasure's Failure (2:1–17, 22–23)

5. Invite class members to follow in their Bibles and look for the failures of wisdom as you read 1:12–18 aloud. Enlist a class member to jot responses on the markerboard as other participants share aloud. (Responses may include heavy burden, chasing after the wind, sorrow, grief.)

6. Read 1:18 again, and point out that this verse seems to capture the Teacher's overall feelings about wisdom. Wisdom can, in fact, deepen our difficulty with meaninglessness and frustration. The more we know, the more we know we don't know! Allow time for discussion.

7. Remind class members that we, like the Teacher in Ecclesiastes, must live with a paradox, for the wisdom of this world is simple folly to God. Invite class members to examine the Beatitudes in Matthew 5. Notice some of the examples of paradox in Matthew 5:3–5:
   - The poor in spirit will receive the kingdom of heaven.
   - Those who mourn will be comforted.
   - The meek will inherit the earth.

Sum up wisdom's failure by saying, *We must guard against the life-long search for earthly wisdom that ends in pointless folly. If we seek God, then wisdom will follow.*

8. Invite participants to follow in their Bibles and listen for the failures of pleasure as you read aloud Ecclesiastes 2:1–17, 22–23. Again, enlist a person to jot responses on the markerboard as other participants share aloud. (Responses may include laughter will soon wear thin, work is futile, collecting possessions and treasures do not bring true happiness, both wise people and fools die.) Point out that in spite of all his achievements, the Teacher despaired about life and questioned whether it had any meaning.

9. Call attention once more to the question of the day, "What is the sense of it all?" Comment that the Teacher gives us a glimpse of the light at the end of the tunnel in Ecclesiastes 3:14. Enlist a participant to read the verse aloud to the class. Share that it is when we fear God (stand in awe of him) that life makes sense.

Encourage Application

10. Ask, *Why do you think all the efforts of the Teacher to find meaning in life failed?*

11. Invite class members to ponder silently the following questions:
    • Do I trust in earthly wisdom, or do I seek God?
    • Do I seek fulfillment in earthly pleasures?
    • Do I allow God to be the center of my life, to bring meaning and purpose?
    • How would I describe my relationship with God?

12. Comment that we live in a time not unlike that of the Teacher, for we all must struggle with life's meaning. We struggle, we strive, we question, we wonder, we laugh, we cry, we seek, and we try. Perhaps along our journey we will, at some point, echo the words of the Apostle Peter in John 6:68, "Lord, to whom shall we go? You have the words of eternal life."

Close in prayer.

Teaching Plan—Lecture and Questions

Connect with Life

1. Share the following true information with your class: In 2004 A.J. Jacobs completed a book about his quest to become the smartest person in the world by reading the entire thirty-two volume set of *Encyclopedia Britannica*. His goals were to join *Mensa* (the organization for people whose IQ is in the top 2% of the population), win a spot on *Jeopardy!*, and absorb 33,000 pages of learning.[3]

2. Ask class members to consider the following questions and share responses aloud with the group:
   • What would you do if you were the smartest person in the world?
   • What are the benefits of knowledge and wisdom?

   Point out that the class will consider ideas about the proper place of wisdom and education near the conclusion of the lesson.

3. Point out that in today's study we will again see that wisdom and knowledge, along with the pleasure they may bring, fall short in themselves of providing meaning for life.

Guide Bible Study

4. Invite class members to follow along as you read Ecclesiastes 1:12–18 aloud. Ask participants to discuss the following questions:
   • What were the Teacher's accomplishments?
   • What had the Teacher seen?
   • What did the Teacher say to himself?
   • What was the Teacher's conclusion?

5. Call attention to the statements the Teacher proclaimed in 1:15. Note that these sayings probably relate directly to the king's expression in verse 14—that it is futile for humans to try to contradict the laws of God expressed in nature. Perhaps ancient Egyptian educators insisted that carpenters could straighten a crooked stick and that a deficit could be turned into a surplus. But the Teacher reminds us that there is no gain at all from this kind of toil.

ECCLESIASTES: Struggling to Find Meaning in Life

6. Read 1:17–18 once more, and suggest the following discussion ideas:
   - Wisdom is not something that can be grasped and controlled.
   - Although wisdom and knowledge are valuable and useful, they paradoxically may bring grief, frustration, and pain.
   - The more we really know about the world we live in, the more we must depend on God.

7. Enlist two class members to share in reading Ecclesiastes 2:1–17. Have one reader to read the odd-numbered verses and the other to read the even-numbered verses. Ask the following discussion questions based on these verses:
   - Where did the Teacher look for pleasure?
   - What kind of treasures did he accumulate?
   - Why didn't this great gathering of possessions bring him pleasure?
   - How might one's senses (sight, smell, etc.) tempt a person to seek fulfillment in pleasure?
   - How are a wise person and a fool different?
   - How are they alike?
   - How did the Teacher feel about life according to 2:17? Why?

8. Read 2:22–23, and comment that they summarize the result of a life lived without a deep regard for God, a life lived in pursuit of merely human wisdom and earthly pleasure.

Encourage Application

9. Ask, *Based on today's Scripture passage, what is the true value of wisdom and education?* Allow time for response, and then direct members to the story of the wise builder in Matthew 7:24–27. Point out the difference between utilizing godly wisdom and seeking worldly wisdom.

10. Comment that perhaps we live in a time when more people aspire to be like the Teacher than ever before. Wisdom is only a computer class away; opportunities for pleasure surround us; possessions can be ours with the mere swipe of a credit card. Remind members that the truly wise person builds his or her house on the rock and seeks God in the midst of every life event and activity.

11. Ask, *Why did the Teacher fail in his quest for meaning in life? How is it possible to find meaning and purpose in life?* The Teacher found the answer, and we will consider it in the next session. Close by reading Ecclesiastes 12:13 (part of next week's focal passage).

NOTES

1. Tyndale House Publishers, Inc., 1971, 1986.

2. John D. Davis, *Davis Dictionary of the Bible,* Fourth Revised Edition (Nashville, Tennessee: Broadman Press, 1977), 800.

3. A. J. Jacobs, *The Know-It-All: One Man's Humble Quest to Become the Smartest Man in the World* (New York: Simon and Schuster, 2004).

Toward a More Meaningful Life

Focal Text

Ecclesiastes 9:7–10; 12:1–8, 13–14

Background

Ecclesiastes 9; 12

Main Idea

We can move toward a greater sense of meaning in life by enjoying appropriately the physical, temporal blessings God provides and by faithfully serving him.

Question to Explore

How much does God want us to enjoy life? How?

Teaching Aim

To lead participants to identify actions they can take to increase their sense of meaning in life

ECCLESIASTES

Struggling to Find Meaning in Life

BIBLE COMMENTS

Understanding the Context

The Teacher was simply living on the wrong side of Easter. No writing in the Old Testament captures the despair of living without Easter quite like the Book of Ecclesiastes.

All the Teacher knew was this life. How bleak that must have been—reward for doing right in this life only, the scales of justice never balanced, no hope for anything beyond this material world. Paraphrasing Ecclesiastes 9:2b the Living Bible says: "That is why men are not more careful to be good but instead choose their own mad course, for they have no hope—there is nothing but death ahead anyway."[1]

Given that all of life is as meaningless as "a puff of smoke," the question is, *How should I live my life?* The Teacher came down to the end of his journey of looking for something that would point to meaning in life. He had found nothing. Ecclesiastes 9:2 expresses the Teacher's problem: "All share a common destiny—the righteous and the wicked, the good and the bad, the clean and the unclean, those who offer sacrifices and those who do not. As it is with the good man, so with the sinner; as it is with those who take oaths, so with those who are afraid to take them." In light

99

of this perspective on life, what should a person do? The answer is *carpe diem!*—seize the day!

Interpreting the Scriptures

God Wants You to Enjoy (9:7–10)

9:7–9. What had previously been stated as advice from the Teacher is now an urgent command: "Go," "eat," "drink," "be clothed," "anoint," "enjoy." Do these things, enjoy life, not because it is a regrettable second best, but because doing so bears God's stamp of approval.

Food, drink, clothing, and family union form a God-given basis for a good life. Pull out all the stops: wear white clothing and anoint your head with oil (symbols of festivity and joy). Fast forward to Revelation 7:9 where a great gathering of people from every nation are ". . . wearing white robes and . . . holding palm branches in their hands. . ." (Revelation 7:9). They are celebrating the salvation that had come to them from God.

9:10. Throw yourself into your work with enthusiasm, whatever your work may be. Why? Because we all have a one-way ticket to *sheol,* the place of the dead, and there no one can work. Jesus might have been paraphrasing this verse when he said to his disciples: "As long as it is day, we must do the work of him who sent me. Night is coming, when no one can work" (John 9:4).

Death is life's most common denominator. The Teacher reminds us that death is no respecter of persons. Death comes to good folk and bad; to those who are faithful in church attendance and to those who never darken the door. The Hebrew word translated "grave" in the phrase "in the grave, where you are going" is the word *sheol.* The NIV also translates it as "pit," "depths," and "death." The King James Version translates the word about half of the time as "grave," and half of the time "hell," with "pit" sprinkled in here and there.

For the Hebrews, *sheol* was not the physical grave, and neither was it a place where the wicked went to be punished. Rather it was a kind of subterranean retreat where all of the dead went. *Sheol* was a gray, featureless place where all that makes life worth living was absent.

That is why the Teacher quotes with approval the proverb, ". . . Even a live dog is better off than a dead lion!" (Ecclesiastes 9:4). To be alive is to have some possibility for tomorrow. In the Hebrew view of *sheol*, death was the end of all that life has to offer. Life and life alone was real. Better to face life with all of its problems and ambiguities than to leap into the dark nothingness of death.

We must remember that the Teacher expressed these sentiments before the resurrection of the Lord Jesus. A world without Jesus being raised from the dead would be bleak indeed, and the Apostle Paul understood this well: "For if there is no resurrection of the dead, then Christ must still be dead. And if he is still dead, then all our preaching is useless and your trust in God is empty, worthless, hopeless; and we apostles are all liars because we have said that God raised Christ from the grave, and of course that isn't true if the dead do not come back to life again. If they don't, then Christ is still dead, and you are very foolish to keep on trusting God to save you, and you are still under condemnation for your sins; in that case, all Christians who have died are lost! And if being a Christian is of value to us only now in this life, we are the most miserable of creatures" (1 Corinthians 15:13–19, The Living Bible).

For Young People: Remember Your Creator (12:1–8)

12:1. God often remembers people to bless them (1 Samuel 1:11, 19–20; Nehemiah 13:31; Psalm 20:3–4). This verse in Ecclesiastes, though, calls us to remember the Creator God so as to reverence and worship him. We are called to remember ". . . in the days of your youth. . . ." Why "remember" when we are young? Because ". . . the days of trouble come . . ." (presumably referring to old age) when there will be no pleasure in one's days (pleasure as in Eccles. 9:7–9).

When a person comes to Christ as a young man or woman, there is a lifetime ahead when he or she can embark joyfully on a life of service to the kingdom. When a person comes to Christ later in life, it is wonderful, but often much opportunity has been lost, frittered away in destructive pursuits.

It might be interesting to do a little survey of your class as to the number of the class who came to a saving knowledge of Christ before they graduated from high school (perhaps in a church camp or Vacation Bible School). These folk often feel overshadowed by those who were saved later in life, perhaps snatched out of the clutches of destructive habits or addictions. Such conversions are wonderful, of course, but greater yet is to be saved *from* ever getting into the snares of a destructive life style.

Vignettes of Old Age (12:2–5a)

The *first picture* (12:2) is of a gathering storm that blots out the heavenly luminaries. It is a persistent storm that will not go away. As long as one may look for clear skies, they are gone.

The *second picture* (12:3–4) is of a once busy estate that has now fallen into decay. In its heyday, it was a virtual beehive of activity. Male and female servants were busy at work. People made social calls to the owners of the estate. Now the gates are closed, and quiet descends. What a picture of the coming of old age.

The *third picture* (12:5) is of an old man who was no longer able to climb a hill, and even a walk in the street caused some thought about the possibility of falling and breaking a bone. Here three phrases describe the life of the old person. Consider one possible understanding for each. First, "... when the almond tree blossoms." The blossoms are a pinkish white, suggesting the white hair of old age. Second, "... the grasshopper drags himself along. . . ." The grasshopper flits easily from stalk to stalk in its insatiable appetite. Here after heavily overeating, the grasshopper finds it difficult to move about, an appropriate image of an older person whose movement is labored. Third, "... desire no longer is stirred." This phrase describes a time when sexual desire has left, never to return.

Death Comes (12:5b–8)

Death strikes, a person goes to his "eternal home," and the professional mourners come for what is just another job to them. Two pictures stress the finality of death, both of which may come from the busy estate in verses 3–4. The first is of an expensive lamp or bowl suspended from the ceiling by a silver chain. Death is the snapping of the chain with the bowl or lamp lying broken on the floor. The second picture is of the well of the estate. To the well, maidens came with their pitchers to draw water from a pulley worked on a wheel. Now, at the well, there is only a broken pitcher beside a broken wheel.

Further, "... the dust returns to the ground it came from, and the spirit returns to God who gave it" (12:7). There remains nothing more to be said. We are back to dust, our beginning described in Genesis 2:7; 3:19. Too, the Teacher is back to where he began, "'Meaningless! Meaningless!' says the Teacher. 'Everything is meaningless!'" (Eccles. 12:8).

It All Comes Down To This (12:13–14)

When it is all said and done, it comes down to this, "...Fear God and keep his commandments....God will bring every deed into judgment...."

These last two verses place the entire book in the context of the faith community of Israel. Perhaps our Teacher backed off, looked at his work, and assumed the posture of a more traditional wisdom teacher. Note the reference "Be warned, my son" (12:12), and compare it to Proverbs 1:8; 2:1; 3:1; 4:10; 5:1; 6:1; 7:1; and similar references. Some Old Testament scholars, though, see the work of our Teacher ending with verse 8, and our last three verses to be the results of a post-exilic wisdom teacher editing this work to fit it in with the faith community of Israel sometime after the return from Babylon.

Focusing on the Meaning

In the movie *The Dead Poet's Society*, private prep school English teacher John Keating, played by Robin Williams, took his class out into the hall and showed them the trophy case where the glory days of the school were enshrined with trophies and pictures of teams of the past. Williams reminded them that once these young men, now gone, were as they were—young, vigorous, with a lifetime ahead of them. Now, he said, they are all dead. Then he asked, "What do you think they would say to you as you embark on this year? Get up close to the glass so you can hear." Then, slipping up behind the boys, he whispered, "*Carpe diem!*" Seize the day!

Our Teacher has told us something similar. How should we live our lives in the light of everything being meaningless? *Carpe diem!* Seize the day! The Teacher had said, "Enjoy life" (9:9; see 9:7–9). Perhaps the popular song of the 1950s, "Enjoy Yourself (It's Later than You Think)," picks up some of the Teacher's theme.[2] The Teacher continued, "Whatever your hand finds to do, do it with all your might..." (9:10). Too, the Teacher concluded, serve God while you can (see 12:1, "Remember your Creator in the days of your youth, before the days of trouble....").

What God created and gave to his children is to be enjoyed. Sometimes we Christians, whose heritage goes back to Puritanism, have problems with the idea of enjoyment. A friend of mine who grew up in a very conservative Christian family of meager means told me, "I remember the first time I tasted ice cream. I just knew that the devil had made it." He went on to say that God made bad-tasting medicine because it was "good for you." Apparently God, for my friend, was about what was only for his children's good and not also what was for their enjoyment. What do you think?

TEACHING PLANS

Teaching Plan—Varied Learning Activities

Connect with Life

1. Place a sentence strip that says "Life means nothing . . ." on the focal wall so that class members can see it during the entire session. Prepare another strip for later use that says ". . . without God."

2. Distribute newspapers to class members, and ask them to identify articles and advertisements related to pleasure and recreation (movies, restaurants, ball game schedules, coffee shops, etc.). (Or you could ask them to name advertisements they have seen and substitute the question in parentheses that follows.) Ask the following awareness questions:
   - How much of the newspaper is devoted to articles and advertisements related to pleasure? (Or, how much emphasis does our society place on pleasure? What evidence can you cite?)
   - Based on previous lessons from Ecclesiastes, should we participate in activities for pleasure? Why or why not?
   - Do you think God is concerned with the pleasure and meaning we find in this world?

Guide Bible Study

3. Call on a class member to read Ecclesiastes 9:7–10. Note that this verse appears to be a contrast from earlier passages in our study. Allow time for discussion. (You may wish to point out that earlier verses in Ecclesiastes convey a similar thought. Read 2:24–25; 3:12–13, 22; 5:18–20; 8:15.) Comment that one should be careful to understand

these verses, for they are not written for those who give no regard for God. Rather, they are written to show that life, for those who have a relationship with God, can have meaning and fulfillment and be fun!

4. Form class members into three small groups (two to six people each). Instruct each group to read Ecclesiastes 12:1–8 and complete the assignment for their group. Allow ten minutes for group activity, and then ask a spokesperson from each group to share findings with the large group. (A copy of the assignments can be downloaded from www.baptistwaypress.org.)

Group 1: Remember

Read Ecclesiastes 12:1–8.
(1) What does "Remember your Creator in the days of your youth" (Eccles. 12:1) mean?
(2) Why is it so important to "remember"?
(3) Can you recall other occasions in the Bible where one is asked to remember?
(4) What are the pitfalls of forgetting?

Group 2: Dreary Days Ahead

Read Ecclesiastes 12:1–8.
(1) How did the Teacher describe "the days of trouble"?
(2) Should the potential of gloom in later years diminish the joy and meaning one can have now? Why or why not?
(3) What do you think about the way the Teacher described "the days of trouble" of later years?

Group 3: Eat, Drink and Be Merry

Read Ecclesiastes 12:1–8.
(1) Read the parable of the barn builder in Luke 12:16–20.
(2) How might Jesus' warning in this passage relate to the Teacher's warning?
(3) How are people tempted to live with wrong motives toward a shallow existence?
(4) How can people avoid yielding to this temptation?

LESSON 9: Toward a More Meaningful Life

5. After group reports, comment that the number of reality television shows today may depict people's desire for adventure, meaning, and purpose in life. We all seem to search for our place, our purpose. Lead participants to read Ecclesiastes 12:13–14 aloud as a group, using the Scripture translation printed in the *Study Guide*.

6. Lead class members to respond to the following discussion questions:
   • How do we "fear God"?
   • How is our obedience (or disobedience) to God a reflection of our love for and trust in him?
   • How can we relate the instruction "Fear God and keep his commandments" in 12:13 to the instructions about enjoying life in 9:7–10?

Encourage Application

7. Direct members to the presentation of spiritual stages under the heading "Remember the Creator of Your Youth" in the *Study Guide* ("As we grow and develop as human beings...."). Encourage each member to consider the model and to examine his or her life in light of these four steps. Invite members to share their thoughts with the group.

8. Call attention to the sentence strip on the focal wall. Add the second strip to the end of the first, making the entire sentence read "Life means nothing . . . without God."

9. Relate the following true story: On October 30, 2005, members and guests of University Baptist Church in Waco, Texas, gathered for Bible study, worship, and the ordinance of baptism. During the baptism ceremony, pastor Kyle Lake reached for a microphone and was immediately electrocuted. Worship band members pulled him from the baptistery, and doctors in attendance rushed to provide medical assistance. Minutes later, among a throng of friends and family members, the emergency room doctor announced that the thirty-three-year-old pastor did not survive. While his death is still a great tragedy to all who knew him, his life was a celebration. Kyle seemed to enjoy every minute of everything he did. In fact, the notes in his Bible for the sermon he was to preach later that morning begin,

Live. And Live Well. BREATHE. Breathe in and Breathe deeply. Be PRESENT. Do not be past. Do not be future. Be now. . . .

The notes conclude:

Feel the SATISFACTION of a job well done—a paper well-written, a project thoroughly completed, a play well-performed. . . . Taste every ounce of flavor. Taste every ounce of friendship. Taste every ounce of Life. Because-it-is-most-definitely-a-Gift.[3]

10. Ask, *How can we enjoy the life God gives us? What does Ecclesiastes say to you about how we can increase our sense of meaning in life?* Allow time for discussion, and then enlist a participant to read John 10:10. Close with prayer.

Teaching Plan—Lecture and Questions

Connect with Life

1. Invite several class members to complete the sentence, "The most meaningful time in my life was when. . . ."

2. Invite several other participants to complete the sentence, "Before I die I want to. . . ."

3. Follow up with the Question to Explore for today's study, "How much does God want us to enjoy life? How?" Allow time for discussion.

Guide Bible Study

4. Call attention to the outline for today's study (you may wish to list the outline on a previously made poster or write it on a markerboard):

> ### Toward a More Meaningful Life
> The Race Is Not Always to the Swift (9:7–10)
> Remember the Creator of Your Youth (12:1–8)
> The Whole Duty of a Person (12:13–14)

5. Enlist a class member to read Ecclesiastes 9:7–10. Invite class members to listen for the instructions the Teacher gave. Then ask the following questions:
   - Do these verses seem to contrast earlier passages we studied in Ecclesiastes? If so, how? (Consider referring also to similar thoughts in Ecclesiastes 2:24–25; 3:12–13, 22; 5:18–20; 8:15.)
   - Do you think these verses were meant primarily for believers? Why or why not?
   - What is the significance of white clothing and abundant oil?
   - How do these verses speak to the relationship with one's spouse?
   - According to these verses, is it okay for God's people to enjoy creation?

6. Invite another member to read Ecclesiastes 12:1–8. Refer to, summarize, and invite comments on the idea of remembering from information in the *Study Guide* under the heading "Remember the Creator of Your Youth (12:1–8)." You may want to point out the following thoughts:
   - God's people are encouraged to "remember" many times in the Book of Deuteronomy (see Deuteronomy 4:10; 5:15; 7:18; 8:2, 18; 9:7, 27; 15:15; 16:3, 12; 24:9, 18, 22; 25:17; 32:7).
   - God's people had completed the Exodus and were perched at the edge of the Promised Land, waiting on God.
   - No doubt many people thought, *There must be more to life than this!*
   - God's people were forgetful!
   - God used these instances to remind people of their plight before God and of his goodness on their behalf.
   - Perhaps one can better trust what God is doing in the present by remembering what God has done in the past.
   - Maybe it is by remembering that we can have hope for the days ahead and have a more meaningful life!
   - Painful consequences naturally show up when we do not "remember."

7. Read Ecclesiastes 12:1–8 again, and lead class members to reflect on the following questions:
   - Why do you think it is important to remember *now*?

- Does the Teacher's tone in these verses tend to make the days ahead look blessed or dreary?
- What do you think the Teacher was trying to say?

8. Read Ecclesiastes 12:13–14 aloud to the class. Point out that this small kernel of truth may well be the key for one to have a meaningful life. It points out what a person is to do (fear God, keep God's commands) and what God will do (judge good and evil deeds).

Encourage Application

9. Call attention to the questions in the *Study Guide*. Encourage participants to respond aloud as each question is considered.

10. Share with participants that to really get to the heart of today's study, we must ask ourselves, *Is my life meaningful? Why or why not? What does Ecclesiastes say to us about how we can have greater meaning in our lives?* Invite responses to the last question.

11. Close in prayer, challenging class members to live the meaningful life to which God calls them!

NOTES

1. *The Living Bible*, second edition (Wheaton, Illinois: Tyndale House Publisher, Inc., 1986).

2. Herb Magidson, "Enjoy Yourself (It's Later than You Think)," 1948. For the words, do an internet search for this title or for Herb Magidson.

3. See www.ubcwaco.org/2004/sermonexcerpt.html.

Focal Text

Habakkuk 1:1—2:4, 15–16

Background

Habakkuk 1—2

Main Idea

God will surely bring justice in our world, although how and when God will do so may not be in accord with our timetable and our desires.

Question to Explore

Can we trust God to bring justice to our world?

Teaching Aim

To lead participants to summarize the conversation between the prophet and God about God's bringing justice and to suggest implications for our world and our day

HABAKKUK

Suffering Injustice

Lesson Ten

How Long, God?

BIBLE COMMENTS

Understanding the Context

We know almost nothing about the prophet Habakkuk. Unlike many prophets in the Old Testament, the book contains no reference about Habakkuk's hometown, father, or family. The prophet's name, "Habakkuk," means *embrace* and may represent a nickname. The name "Habakkuk" also appears in the Apocryphal work Bel and the Dragon (verses 33–39 in that book).

The prophet Habakkuk "saw"[1] a "burden" that led him to complain to Yahweh.[2] The book contains language typical of Old Testament laments. The laments in the Book of Habakkuk may indicate the prophet's official intercession for the community. The prophet Habakkuk sensed a heavy responsibility to intercede on behalf of his community that suffered.

Additionally, several passages appear to contain musical directions (Habakkuk 3:1, 3, 9, 13, 19), which indicates that Israel may have used this material in its worship liturgy. Based on the contents of the book, it is possible that the prophet exercised responsibilities in the temple worship in Jerusalem. However, intercession alone does not indicate that the prophet was a cultic official. For instance, Amos interceded for the people (Amos 7:1–6), but he was not a cultic prophet.

Internal evidence from the book provides clues for the date of composition. Habakkuk 1:6 states that Yahweh was "rousing the Chaldeans, that fierce and impetuous nation, who march through the breadth of the earth to seize dwellings not their own." The name "Chaldeans" first appears in the ninth century B.C. in reference to a group of tribes in southern Mesopotamia. Biblical texts use the term to refer primarily to ancient scholars such as the priests, magicians, astrologers, and diviners in southern Mesopotamia and secondarily to the Babylonians in general.[3]

Nabopolasar, who ruled the Assyrian province of Babylon, declared independence from Assyria in 626 B.C. Under his leadership and that of his capable son Nebuchadrezzar (sometimes translated Nebuchadnezzar), the newly established kingdom began to sweep across what remained of the declining Assyrian Empire. The Babylonians destroyed the Assyrian city of Nineveh in 612 B.C. Shortly afterwards, King Josiah of Judah died in battle fighting the Egyptians, who had marched through the Valley of Megiddo on the way to fight against the Babylonian army to the north.

Nebuchadrezzar eventually defeated the Assyrians and the Egyptians, reaching Israel in 605 B.C. By 603 B.C., the Babylonians controlled the region of Philistia along the Mediterranean coast. The inhabitants of Judah soon rebelled against the new despot, which led Nebuchadrezzar to lead a punitive campaign against Judah. In March 597 B.C., the Babylonians seized the city of Jerusalem and forcefully deported many of her leading citizens to the suburbs of the city of Babylon, including Judah's youthful King Jehoiachin and the prophet Ezekiel. This deportation removed the "basket of good figs" (Jeremiah 24) from the land. Nebuchadrezzar appointed Zedekiah as king. Zedekiah at first remained loyal to the Babylonians. However, the inhabitants of Jerusalem soon convinced their king to rebel against Babylon. Nebuchadrezzar reacted quickly and with vengeance.

The Babylonian armies captured and destroyed numerous towns and villages throughout the province of Judah in 588 B.C. The actual siege of the city of Jerusalem began in early 588 B.C. and continued until August of 587 or 586 B.C. King Zedekiah had failed to prepare the city for a long siege, and soon conditions in the city deteriorated. Starvation, disease, and death made conditions unbearable in the city. When the Babylonians breached the walls of the city, Zedekiah and his nobles escaped and fled toward the Transjordan. The Babylonians captured them near Jericho. The

Babylonians executed his sons and carried him to Babylon. The Babylonians systematically destroyed Jerusalem and burned the temple. The
destruction was complete.

Therefore, the book appears to reflect the struggles of the people of
Judah between Josiah's death (609 b.c.) and the deportation in 597 b.c.
If this is the setting, then the prophet may have been a contemporary of
Zephaniah, Jeremiah, and Nahum. From the historical background and
the context of the book, we can safely conclude that the prophet Habakkuk was active in Judah at the end of the seventh and the beginning of the
sixth centuries b.c.

Interpreting the Scriptures

Round One (1:2–11)

The Problem (1:2–4)

How long must the prophet witness violence and wickedness? Twice in
the opening verses (Hab. 1:2, 3) the prophet used an expression that means
"violence." This is the opposite of Yahweh's "justice" (1:4). The prophet
complained of the moral evils that lead to "strife and contention" (1:3),
which indicate a breakdown in human relationships. The strong oppressed
the weak. Litigation that arose from personal feuds against others governed behavior. Public quarrels and endless nagging over various issues
distracted people from the "law" (torah[4]) of Yahweh (1:4). "The wicked" in
verse 4 refers to the evil people within Judah.[5]

The Hebrew term mishpat, often translated as "justice," occurs twice
in verse 4 and signifies that Yahweh ordained order for the society of the
covenant people.[6] Habakkuk complained that the people of Judah had
abandoned God's intended order for society. A decade earlier, the people
of Judah had participated in a religious reform under the leadership of
King Josiah. God prefers torah, which conveys Israel's entire religious
tradition.[7] The people of Judah had abandoned the torah. According to
the prophet Jeremiah, a contemporary of Habakkuk, even the priests had
ignored the torah.[8] The people preferred the empty pronouncements of
the false prophets.[9] The abandonment of justice led to chaos, the opposite
of Yahweh's order.

God's Answer (1:5–11)

1:5. God answered the complaints Habakkuk raised in verses 2–4. Yahweh hears the persistent prayers of the faithful.[10] Sometimes God's answers to prayers are comforting. Sometimes God's answers to prayers are confounding, as in this section. In a world where God seemed to be an absent deity, Yahweh assured Habakkuk that the deity was at work. God's goal would prevail. God does not sleep nor slumber. Yahweh was not ignorant of what was happening in the world.

1:6. The reference to "Chaldeans" refers to the Babylonians in general. Babylon, led by Nebuchadrezzar, would judge the wicked in Judah. Yahweh informed the prophet, "I am rousing the Chaldeans" to rise in power and to conquer the Near East of Habakkuk's day.

1:7–11. Yahweh described the character of the Babylonians. They inspired fear wherever they went (1:7). Their army devoured the enemy like a vulture that sweeps upon the prey (1:8). They inflicted violence everywhere they traveled (1:9). They obliterated every fortified city they encountered (1:10).

Judah had rejected Yahweh's justice (1:4), which defined order in society. Therefore, Yahweh would impose the Babylonian order on Judah (1:7). Judah chose violence (1:2), and so the Lord would unleash the violence of the Babylonians on the land (1:9). Judah had rejected the instruction of God (1:4), and now Judah would serve the god of Babylonian might.

Round Two (1:12—2:4)

The Problem (1:12—2:1)

Habakkuk had a problem with the response Yahweh gave in 1:5–11. How could a righteous God use the wicked (Babylonians) to punish those (Israel) more righteous than the wicked? Although Judah was wicked, Habakkuk viewed the Babylonians as more wicked.

1:12. For the prophet, it was inconceivable that God would permit evil to triumph. He knew Yahweh as "my God," "my Holy One," and "Rock." These expressions indicate that the prophet was in intimate communion with God.

1:13. The prophet took for granted that God is just, which created an ethical quandary for him. If Yahweh was "pure," then how could Yahweh remain silent when evil triumphed over good? "The wicked" refers to either the wicked in Judah or the Babylonians.

1:14–17. These verses point out the vulnerability of humanity to evil in the world. The enemy possess the ability to seize the righteous. The prophet used the metaphors of a fisherman's hook, a net, and a seine to describe how the wicked enrich themselves with the destruction of the righteous. The methods used by the wicked to destroy the righteous become their gods. Habakkuk struggled with the paradox that a righteous God would allow the wicked to continue the devastation of the righteous.

2:1. Habakkuk continued his intimate communion with God in spite of the perceived contradictions in God's actions. He also felt a strong sense of responsibility for his community. The language of battle in God's speech (1:5–11) elicited a military response by Habakkuk. He would "keep watch" as though he stood guard on the walls of a fortress facing attack. The prophet would wait for a response from God to his complaint.

God's Answer (2:2–4)

2:2. Eventually, Yahweh answered Habakkuk by means of a vision. The Lord instructed the prophet, "Write the vision." Oral communication was easily altered if circumstances changed. However, when the message was put in writing, the message was either true or false, depending on the faithfulness of the message to the actual events. God's message to the prophet would not change. The Babylonians would attack as the instruments of God's judgment on the wicked in the land of Judah. Yes, God would use an evil empire to judge the covenant people. The "runner" refers to a courier who delivered the message to the assigned destinations.

2:3. The message refers to the "end" and was not a threat. What Yahweh had promised "will surely come" to pass. God warned the prophet not to interpret a delay in the implementation as a sign that God had had a change of heart.

2:4. Yahweh promised that a righteous remnant would survive the certain judgment of God at the hand of the Babylonians. This verse emphasizes the concept that "the righteous live by their faith" (or faithfulness). By these words, God offered hope for the faithful who lived in the period between the promises and the fulfillment of the promises.

The Apostle Paul relied on verse 4 as he proclaimed justification by faith (Romans 1:17). The reformer, Martin Luther, discovered Paul's message about justification by faith, which helped to shape the Protestant Reformation. Even the author of the Epistle to the Hebrews found the Book of Habakkuk of great significance (Hebrews 10:36–39).

Woes Heaped On Babylon (2:5–20)

Suggestions for the identity of the oppressor in this passage include a Babylonian, an Assyrian, or King Jehoiakim. The identity of the oppressor in the woes remains a mystery, though. The woes apply to any situation of oppression, greed, and idolatry. The Lord declares that the oppressor of the righteous deserves the taunts delivered against him.

The prophet delivered five woes or taunts against those who promote evil, greed, and oppression. The first woe (Hab. 2:6b–8) condemns the person who takes that which belongs to others. The second woe (2:9–11) dooms those who get their wealth by illegal methods. The third woe (2:12–14) condemns the person who runs roughshod over anyone who gets in the way. The fourth woe (2:15–17) dooms those who destroy the lives of others by strong drink. The wicked use strong drink, immorality, and crime for their personal pleasure. The fifth woe (2:18–19) condemns idolatry as worship of fabricated idols.

Focusing on the Meaning

The people of God always sense an obligation to intercede on behalf of those who suffer. People who face mental, physical, and spiritual pain live too close to these events in their lives and need individuals like Habakkuk to intercede before God on their behalf. The existence of injustice in the world demands that we speak out when we observe injustice.

Intercession is tough and requires a willingness to express one's concerns honestly. Anger, frustration, and impatience are human emotions when injustice prevails. Prayer warriors against injustice demonstrate the stamina to complain or confess to God the human emotions experienced by those who suffer.

Faithful people must live in a world as it is. They grow weary of the evil ways of the world. Some individuals take the word of God and twist it to their own selfish purpose. Others break every code of decency and morality, and yet seek to justify their evil. Some cheat, deceive, and lie, and yet are honored in the eyes of society. Habakkuk expressed a weariness of the world of his day.

What is the world coming to? Anyone who has asked that question can identify with Habakkuk. How can anyone experience blessings on this earth in the face of such overwhelming human sin and evil? The Book of Habakkuk takes the reader down the road of doubt to faith. In the end, only those who remain faithful to God have any chance of survival. We can find comfort in the words of the living God, "But the LORD is in his holy temple; let all the earth keep silence before him!" (Hab. 2:20).

TEACHING PLANS

Teaching Plan—Varied Learning Activities

Connect with Life

1. Think of and share a frustrating experience of waiting that you have had (such as ordering something and waiting and waiting for it to arrive, then receiving the wrong thing, and so on; being put on hold for ages on the telephone; or waiting in traffic when you have an important appointment). Ask: *Do you have a "waiting" experience to share with the class?*

Guide Bible Study

2. Use information in "Introducing Habakkuk: Suffering Injustice" in the *Study Guide* and in "Understanding the Context" in this *Teaching Guide* to introduce the study of Habakkuk. Write on the board the title of today's lesson, "How Long, God?"

3. Form the class into two study groups of two to six people each. (If your class is larger than twelve, form additional groups, and give duplicate assignments.) Allow the members to choose to study and interpret the lesson in a creative listening group or a creative arts group. Explain that both groups will make a presentation to the class

HABAKKUK: Suffering Injustice

at the end of the group time of about twenty minutes. (Have needed supplies available. The creative listening group will need paper and pencils. The creative arts group will need a variety of art supplies: paper, pencils, crayons or makers, scissors, colored paper, yarn, glue.) Print each group's assignments on an index card (download a copy from www.baptistwaypress.org). Give the assignment to someone you feel can best lead the group. (Enlisting group leaders ahead of time will allow them to be prepared to make suggestions.)

Guidance for Leader of Creative Listening Group on Habakkuk's Laments (Hab. 1:2–4; 1:12—2:1)

Tell the group: Our assignment is to explore today's Scriptures in the following way. I will read Habakkuk's first lament (Hab.1:1–4) to you twice. The first time, listen attentively, hearing every word. Get the flow of the story. The second time, listen for the complaints Habakkuk had against God. Write down what you hear.

Repeat the same procedure with Habakkuk's second complaint (1:12—2:1.)

Then lead the group to share and discuss answers and to prepare summary statements of Habakkuk's laments to report to the class.

Guidance for Leader of Creative Arts Group on God's Answers to Habakkuk (Hab.1:5–11; 2:2–20)

Tell the group: Our assignment is to explore today's Scriptures in the following way. Read 1:5–11 and 2:2–20 silently. Then, using the art materials available, write a poem or brief story, draw a picture, create an art work, or write a simple song that illustrates God's answers. You can work as individuals or in pairs. We will share our work together as a group and then choose several of the creations to present to the class at report time.

4. Reassemble the class, and invite each group to share its work. Follow the order of the Scriptures (Lament, Answer, Lament, Answer).

5. Refer to 2:6–20. Use the information in the section in the *Study Guide* titled "Five Woes of the Oppressed" and the section in this *Teaching Guide* titled "Woes Heaped on Babylon" to explain Habakkuk's description of the woes that would befall those who oppressed others.

Encourage Application

6. Ask: *What did Habakkuk learn from his dialogue with God? In what ways could he feel that justice was done? How can this study help us to know that we can trust God to bring justice to our world and deal with the problems we see?*

7. Close with prayer, thanking God that we can voice our complaints and concerns to him. Thank God for Scripture that teaches us how others centuries ago wrestled with problems similar to those we have today. Conclude with Habakkuk's beautiful declaration in 2:20: "The Lord is in his holy temple; let all the earth be silent before him."

Teaching Plan—Lecture and Questions

Connect with Life

1. Write this question on the board: "What are some things we wait for?"

2. Greet each person as he or she comes into the room, inviting everyone to write responses underneath. Encourage comments and informal discussion about their responses. Ask: *Why do we dislike waiting?*

Guide Bible Study

3. Point out that today's lesson is entitled, "How Long, God?" Explain that Habakkuk was waiting for God's response to several complaints.

4. Give a brief introduction to the Book of Habakkuk using the article in the *Study Guide* titled "Introducing Habakkuk."

5. In advance, engage two readers to read the dialogue between Habakkuk and God, asking the readers to become familiar with the text beforehand so they can read it with ease. State that our lesson today will be presented as an informal dialogue between God and Habakkuk, with class discussion to follow each act. The readers should stand or sit in front of the class. They need to read from the same

Bible translation. (Download from www.baptistwaypress.org a dramatic reading based on this passage.)

Dialogue of Habakkuk and God (Habakkuk 1—2)

Act One

Habakkuk: Read Habakkuk 1:2–4.
God: Read Habakkuk 1:5–11.

6. Ask: *Why did God's response surprise Habakkuk? In what way does it surprise you? How does Habakkuk describe Judah's moral condition? What parallels might we infer to present-day situations in the world?*

7. Continue the reading.

Act Two

Habakkuk: Read Habakkuk 1:12—2:1.
God: Read Habakkuk 2:2–4.

8. Using the information in the *Study Guide*, explain how the statement in 2:4, "the righteous will live by his faith," was understood in Habakkuk's day, and how the Apostle Paul used it (Romans 1:17).

9. Then read the woes stated in Habakkuk 2:6, 9, 12, 15–16, 19. Explain the significance of these five woes, using information in the *Study Guide* and in "Bible Comments" in this *Teaching Guide.*

Encourage Application

10. Lead the class to respond to these questions:
    * How would you summarize Habakkuk's question to God?
    * How would you summarize God's answer to Habakkuk?
    * How would you summarize Habakkuk's response?
    * What are some implications for us?
    * Will you share a story about a time in your life when God answered a request after a long wait?

11. Close with prayer, thanking God that he is in control of human affairs and asking him to remind us often that his justice ultimately will prevail.

NOTES

1. Unless otherwise indicated, all Scripture quotes in lessons 10–11 on Habakkuk are from the New Revised Standard Version.

2. Yahweh or YHWH is the sacred name of God in the Old Testament. Most English translations translate it as LORD.

3. Grant Frame, "Chaldeans," *The Oxford Encyclopedia of Archaeology in the Near East*, vol. 1, ed. Eric M. Meyers (New York: Oxford University Press, 1997), 1:482–483.

4. *Torah* refers to Yahweh's instructions, which maintain orderliness in society.

5. Elizabeth Achtemeier, *Nahum—Malachi* (Atlanta, GA: John Knox Press, 1986), 32.

6. Achtemeier, *Nahum—Malachi*, 34. Isaiah 42:1–4 and Jeremiah 5:1–9 indicate the same idea for *mishpat*.

7. Achtemeier, *Nahum—Malachi*, 34.

8. Jer. 2:8.

9. Jer. 23:9–40.

10. See Luke 18:1–8.

Habakkuk 3:1–2, 12–19

Background

Habakkuk 3

Main Idea

Faith enables us to wait for God even when the circumstances are difficult and our patience is running out.

Question to Explore

How does your faith in God help you when you face difficult circumstances?

Teaching Aim

To lead adults to describe the actions of God and the prophet and to identify implications for us as we wait on God to bring us help

HABAKKUK

Suffering Injustice

Lesson Eleven

Faith Regardless

BIBLE COMMENTS

Understanding the Context

Habakkuk 3 contains the prophet's psalm of faith. Chapters 1 and 2 present several complaints to and about Yahweh. With each complaint, the Lord responded to the prophet. The first response from God (1:5–11) did not satisfy Habakkuk, who then complained about Yahweh's answer. The Lord's second response (2:2–20) apparently provided the assurance Habakkuk required. The brief account of Habakkuk's debate with God may have gone back-and-forth for several rounds before Yahweh's answer in chapter 2. The debate in chapters 1 and 2 indicates that honest doubt is a true religious attitude and that the Lord does not condemn the faithful for expressing honest emotions.

Laments in the Old Testament often end in a hymn of praise or thanksgiving for the Lord's salvation. The literary structure of the Book of Habakkuk also includes a hymn following the laments in the first two chapters. This structure—lament and praise—reminds the faithful that the Lord does listen to the deepest human emotions and that we need to offer to the Lord our praise for his response.

The autobiographical statements in 3:2 and 3:16 frame the hymn presented in 3:3–15. These statements also connect the hymn of chapter 3 with the events presented in chapters 1—2. Yahweh declared that the spirit of the proud "is not right in them" (Habakkuk 2:4a). Furthermore, the proud will perish, but "the righteous live by their faith" (Hab. 2:4b). The series of taunts (2:6–20) proclaim that the sins of the wicked will return on the wicked to destroy them. Knowledge of God's judgment led the prophet to "stand in awe" (3:2a). The prophet could only pray for mercy before the work of God.

Interpreting the Scriptures

Introduction to Habakkuk's Psalm (3:1)

Verse 1 introduces the prayer of Habakkuk in 3:2 and the psalm or hymn that follows. In the superscription contained in this verse, the word "Shigionoth" is obscure, but it may refer to a type of liturgical instruction. The term also occurs in Psalm 7 in an equally obscure setting. The context in both passages may indicate some type of musical instruction. The Book of Habakkuk ends with a reference to "the choirmaster: with stringed[1] instruments" (author's translation), which supports the musical interpretation of "Shigionoth." Verse 1 is generally interpreted as a later superscription to the hymn that gives liturgical direction for its use in worship in the temple.

Habakkuk's Hymn and Prayer (3:2–15)

This hymn is set within an autobiographical framework. It begins with a prayer and ends in a prayer.

3:2. The prayer is Habakkuk's response to the answer of Yahweh given in 2:2–20. The prophet proclaimed that he had heard the report of the Lord. The next phrase explains what it means to hear of God's renown. The faithful always stand in "awe" of the work of God. The word translated as "awe" refers to standing in *fear* when confronted with the work of Yahweh.

The prophet called on the Lord to "revive" the divine work in his own day. For the prophet the divine work would be revived only when God caused it to be known. Neither the prophet nor the people could revive or make God's work known. We can only respond to the work of the Lord.

Habakkuk understood that the revival of God's work in his day would mean judgment. Therefore, the prophet called on God to remember to show mercy when God made known the divine work. Compassion, even in judgment, is part of the character of God.

The Hymn (3:3–15)

Israel often sang hymns in worship. This hymn is not just an aural revelation, something that is heard. It is a vision in which the prophet saw Yahweh's judgment on the Babylonians. Indeed, all the nations of the earth would experience the divine judgment (3:12).

The hymn envisions Yahweh's final reckoning with the wicked and the establishment of a new order on the earth. God's *torah* will triumph (1:4). The hymn proclaims the prophet's conviction that judgment "will not delay" (2:3b).

Habakkuk 3:2, 16 express the prophet's strong belief in and reaction to the promises of 2:4, 5–6a, and 6b–20. The hymn (3:3–15) proclaims that God will establish a righteous kingdom on the earth, a promise implied in 2:3. The hymn also confirms the answer that the prophet sought in Habakkuk 1—2. The final autobiographical confession in 3:16–19 demonstrates that the vision stilled the prophet's complaints presented in 1:1–4, 12—2:1.

The hymn contains elements of a prophetic description of a theophany.[2] The passage contains many features of theophanies found elsewhere in the Old Testament. See Deuteronomy 33:2; Judges 5:4–5; Psalm 18:7–15 (parallel to 2 Samuel 22:8–16); Psalms 68:7–8, 17, 32–34; 77:16–19; 97:1–5. The similarities to other theophanies may indicate that the hymn was an independent work used in Israel's worship. Additionally, the superscription (Hab. 3:1) and postscript (3:19d) attest to the hymn's usage in Israel's worship.

God Comes from the South (3:3–8)

God granted to Habakkuk the privilege of seeing a vision in answer to the prophet's prayer (3:2). God had granted to Moses the opportunity to look into the Promised Land (Deut. 34:1–4). The Lord also allowed Peter, James, and John to see a vision of the glorified Jesus on the Mount of Transfiguration (Mark 9:2–8). Habakkuk's vision brought comfort and reassurance to the prophet that Yahweh was at work.

3:3. The vision begins with God coming from the south marching northward. God had come up from the Sinai with Israel as their King in the period of the Exodus. Now the prophet saw God coming up again from the south, but this time as King over all the earth. The Lord received praise for this march. "Praise" of Yahweh fills the heavens and the earth.

3:4. Habakkuk described the praise and glory of Yahweh as a bright light that dominated the view of God. Rays, like those of the sun, proceeded from God. The prophet emphasized the word "his" in the expression "his hand." The idea is that power goes forth from the hand of God and no one else. The brightness of God's power is but the outskirt of God's true power.

3:5. Enemies fell before the brightness of God as if struck by pestilence and plague, two phenomena of the ancient world over which people had no control.

3:6. Yahweh stood and looked upon the nations. Actually, Yahweh *measured* the nations, that is, sized up the nations for judgment, and caused the nations to "tremble." Majestic mountains "were shattered" along God's path as if to bow before the King of all the earth. Eternal hills, possibly ancient cultic places, bowed as the Lord of creation passed by.

3:7. The hymn uses Cushan and Midian synonymously in this verse, a possible reference to Yahweh's judgments presented in Judges 3:8–10 and Numbers 31:7–8. The Lord ultimately defeated the enemies (Hab. 3:8–15).

3:8. The verse possibly recalls several events associated with God's salvation: (1) turning the Nile River to blood (Exodus 7:17–24); (2) parting the Sea in Exodus (Exod. 14:16, 22, 29); and (3) cutting off the waters of the Jordan (Joshua 3:16). The series of questions are rhetorical. God had subdued the waters long ago.

The final battle (3:9–15)

Yahweh came to conquer the evil that concerned Habakkuk in chapters 1—2. The hymn symbolizes evil as the chaos at creation. Yahweh came as the Divine Warrior to fight the final battle.

3:9. The meaning of the Hebrew text of verse 9 is unclear. The verse appears to proclaim that Yahweh makes the battle bow ready for use. Verse 11 presents the arrows of Yahweh flying in battle.

3:9c–11. Yahweh called on creation to assist in the battle. The rivers split the earth. The mountains shook. The deep bellowed. The sun and moon withheld their light. The arrows from Yahweh's bow (3:9) pierced the darkness, the chaos of evil. The only light seen came from the arrows and spears of God that defeated the evil in the world.

3:12. Yahweh tramples the enemies as one treads the grain (see Isaiah 63:1–6). God trampled on the earth as a punishment of the wicked.

3:13. Yahweh fought the battle described in Habakkuk 3:9–15 to bring salvation to those who trust in him and who are the covenant people. The reference to "your people" parallels "your anointed," which often refers to the Davidic king. In the context of verse 13, it is "your people" who represent the anointed of Yahweh. God will save his anointed ones. However, some scholars doubt the genuineness of the temporal reference to "your anointed" in this verse, since Jehoiakim, an evil king, ruled Judah during the prophet's day. It is certainly possible that Habakkuk's vision of the kingdom included a Davidic ruler, though.

The fate of the wicked was gruesome. "From foundation to roof" refers to laying the wicked open from thigh to neck.

3:14. Yahweh caused a panic among the enemies of the faithful. Enemy warriors were so confused that they attacked their own leaders. Weapons intended for use against the covenant people fell on the enemy themselves. God saved the "poor who were in hiding" (Hab. 3:14). Yet, this salvation might come just as the enemy was ready to devour the righteous, described in the verse as the "poor."

Encouragement in the Knowledge of God's Power (3:16–19)

These verses along with verse 1 form an autobiographical framework for the psalm/hymn that is contained in verses 2–15. Verses 16–19 give Habakkuk's final prayer.

3:16. The vision has come to an end. The prophet returned to the reality of his world. He raised no more questions. His world had not changed. The last part of verse 16 contains a specific reference to the Babylonians of chapter 1. Violence still existed (1:2). "Strife and contention" (1:3) still governed society. The wicked still "surround the righteous" (1:4). The arrogant still acted treacherously (2:5). The poor still suffered at the hands of the powerful (2:6–7). People continued to worship false gods (1:11; 2:18–19).

Now, though, Habakkuk possessed an understanding he did not have before his round of complaints to God. God was indeed at work, unseen, in the midst of the chaos of the human condition. God had granted to Habakkuk a vision to see the final scene in history.

3:17–19c. Habakkuk's song of trust has at least three possible interpretations. First, the song may address the invasion of the Babylonians as presented in Jeremiah 5:17. If so, Habakkuk expressed confidence in Yahweh's salvation. Second, the song may describe the effect of Yahweh's covenant curse on the land (see Amos 4:9; Micah 6:15; Haggai 2:16–17). If so, Habakkuk expressed confidence that Yahweh would save the faithful while judging the wicked. Third, the passage may refer to the Day of the Lord as presented in Joel 1:10–12. If so, Habakkuk expressed confidence that Yahweh would save the faithful on that day.

The first interpretation appears to fit the context of the book and focuses the reader's attention on the invasion by the Babylonians. Habakkuk must live "in the meantime." Evil from the prophet's own people continued in Habakkuk's day. Yet, before the final defeat of evil, Habakkuk must live through the days of the Babylonian attack on Judah.

3:18. Habakkuk proclaimed that come what may, he would "exult in the God of my salvation." He would not allow injustice or violence to deter his trust in the Lord. He would not permit foreign influences (the Babylonians) to discourage his confidence in Yahweh. He would not even allow the hardship of God's destruction of the wicked to shake his faith in God.

3:19a-c. Habakkuk proclaimed that Yahweh was his "strength" or his *army*. He proclaimed that God had set his "feet like the feet of a deer." Roe deer once lived along the treacherous cliffs in the Judean wilderness where one misstep would lead to certain death. Yahweh has ordained that Habakkuk must live in the present, which is treacherous, and not on the safe level plateaus or in the valleys where the journey is smooth. Habakkuk could not choose the path on which he traveled in life. However, God had given to Habakkuk the ability to travel the treacherous path with the sure-footed confidence of a roe deer.

3:19d. The postscript, "To the leader with stringed instruments," constitutes a later addition to the book. It gives us insight into how the ancient Israelites might have used the hymn of Habakkuk in temple worship.

Focusing on the Meaning

The kingdom of God is the church's proper concern. The kingship of the Lord must remain the focus of God's people. The servants of the Lord should not permit the defeat of worthy causes to stop the advancement of the kingdom of God. National upheavals need not make life uncertain. The suffering borne by the children of God will not prevent the advancement of God's work. The Lord's banner will continue to wave proudly. The goal of every church is to fill the earth "with the knowledge of the glory of the LORD, as the waters cover the sea." (Hab. 2:14) The prayer of Habakkuk should be the prayer of the church—*O Lord, renew your work in our time.* We should pray as our Lord taught us: "Your kingdom come. Your will be done, on earth as it is in heaven" (Matthew 6:10).

Yet, the work of human hands can never usher in the kingdom of God. Only God can establish the kingdom in the hearts and souls of sinful humanity. Only God can transform individuals and societies into followers of the Lord of all the earth. We can promote the kingdom. We can oppose the kingdom. But only God has the power to grant the kingdom.

Although God comes to judge, God's arrival will mean salvation (Hab. 3:13a) to those who "stand in awe" (3:2) of the work of the Lord. Jesus proclaimed, "I came that they may have life, and have it abundantly" (John 10:10).

The arrival of God always involves the removal of the wicked, what the Old Testament refers to as the "unclean." The opposite of "holy" is "unclean" and all that is unclean must be removed before the Lord establishes the kingdom. The Bible refers to the removal of all that is "unclean" as judgment. In Habakkuk's day, God's judgment came by the hands of the wicked Babylonians. When God judges the wicked, the righteous may suffer, but the righteous will also be saved by their faith when judgment ends.

TEACHING PLANS

Teaching Plan—Varied Learning Activities

Connect with Life

1. Before class begins, write this statement on the board or a poster board:

Things we wait for:	
Good	Bad

Instruct the members to think of at least one answer for each category and share it with someone sitting near them. After a few minutes, invite volunteers to share their answer with the class. Use these questions to guide discussion: *Is it easier to wait for something good or something bad? Which requires more faith?*

2. In advance, enlist one or two members who enjoy talking to people to prepare a "Faith Report" by interviewing five or ten people, asking these questions: *What is your definition of faith? In what do you have faith?* Encourage the interviewer to find non-churched people as well as church attenders and known Christian friends, and to choose a variety of ages, genders, and ethnicities. Interviews should be short, casual, friendly—not invasive or personal. The interviewer(s) should maintain the anonymity of the people interviewed. Call for the "Faith Report" now. Allow class members to ask questions or reflect on the meaning they find in this survey.

Guide Bible Study

3. Before class time, prepare the following vocabulary matching activity (download from www.baptistwaypress.org). Give each person a worksheet and make clear that *this is not a test!* Encourage the group to complete the matching activity, perhaps in pairs. After a few minutes,

share the correct answers, allowing questions and discussion. Explain that these terms and ideas are in today's lesson but are not words we ordinarily use in conversation, except perhaps "faith."

Vocabulary Matching Worksheet

Instructions: Choose the definition for each of the following words, and write its letter in the blank.

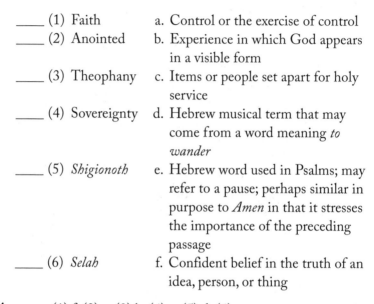

____ (1) Faith	a. Control or the exercise of control
____ (2) Anointed	b. Experience in which God appears in a visible form
____ (3) Theophany	c. Items or people set apart for holy service
____ (4) Sovereignty	d. Hebrew musical term that may come from a word meaning *to wander*
____ (5) *Shigionoth*	e. Hebrew word used in Psalms; may refer to a pause; perhaps similar in purpose to *Amen* in that it stresses the importance of the preceding passage
____ (6) *Selah*	f. Confident belief in the truth of an idea, person, or thing

Answers: (1) f; (2) c; (3) b; (4) a; (5) d; (6) e.

4. Call on someone to read aloud Habakkuk 3:1–2. Explain that these verses begin a prayer, evidently to be sung. Try it! Enlist a singer to improvise a simple melody to the words of verse 2, while others choose one note and hum softly in the background until the soloist is finished. Repeat several times, so that all can gain confidence and join in.

5. Divide the class into two study groups,[3] explaining that each group will explore Habakkuk's personal experience with and response to God. (Download assignments from www.baptistwaypress.org.)

Group 1: Study and report on Habakkuk's vision or theophany (an experience in which God appears in visible form) in Habakkuk 3:3–15, using information in the section "Habakkuk's Theophany" in the *Study Guide.*

Group 2: Explore Habakkuk's response to the theophany (What did he learn?) in Habakkuk 3:16–19, using information in the section "Habakkuk's Confidence" in the *Study Guide.*

6. Give the groups about ten minutes to read and discuss their topics. Then have each group share its findings with the class.

Encourage Application

7. Ask: *What have we learned about Habakkuk?* (Possible answers: creative—a writer and musician; spiritually sensitive; loved God and his nation deeply; a student of history; teachable; a person of faith; etc.) Use these questions to guide further discussion and application:
   • What do we learn from Habakkuk about how God deals with people?
   • In what ways will your faith be different after studying Habakkuk's trial of faith?
   • How can we apply what we learn from Habakkuk's expression of faith in God?

   Close with prayer.

Teaching Plan—Lecture and Questions

Connect with Life

1. Share with the class: *Because today's lesson continues the story of Habakkuk's trial of faith, let's begin by thinking about the journey of faith today.* Ask whether anyone recalls the story in the *Study Guide* about the writer's trial of faith (under the heading "Habakkuk's Confidence"). Invite someone to tell the story. Fill in the information as needed.

Guide Bible Study

2. In advance, write this outline on the board (or write each heading as the lesson progresses.)

Faith Regardless
Habakkuk's Prayer (3:1–2)
Habakkuk's Theophany (3:3–15)
Habakkuk's Confidence (3:16–19)

---

3. Call on someone to read Habakkuk 3:1–2 to the class. Explain that Habakkuk 3 was actually a song set to a musical form of that day called a "*shigionoth.*" Explain "*shigionoth.*" Include an explanation of the use of the term "*Selah*" (3:3). Enlist someone else to read 3:1–2 in a different translation. Ask: *What did Habakkuk want God to do?* (See 3:2.) *Do you think Habakkuk believed that God would do it? What evidence for your answer do you see in these verses? How do past experiences with God help us have faith for the future?*

4. Refer to the heading "Habakkuk's Theophany." Explain the word "theophany" using information in the *Study Guide.* Refer to these examples from Scripture (also listed in the endnote in the *Study Guide*): God was seen as smoke and fire (Genesis 15:17), a fire (Exodus 3:2), a pillar or cloud and a pillar of fire (Exod. 13:17–22), and lightning (Revelation 4:5).

   Have the class read silently Habakkuk 3:3–11, looking for Habakkuk's descriptions of God's appearance in his theophany. Ask, *How did God's presence manifest itself? How did God demonstrate his power?* Review the various ways God manifested himself in this passage of Scripture.

5. Explain the agricultural metaphor in verse 12. Ask, *Why would the people in Habakkuk's day have related to this example?* (They were an agricultural people.) Explain the word "anointed" in verse 13, using information in the *Study Guide.*

6. Call on someone to read aloud Habakkuk 3:16–18 while the class listens for Habakkuk's response to the theophany. Ask, *What was Habakkuk's physical response to the theophany? How would you have responded if this theophany had happened to you? What was Habakkuk's final resolve as a result of this experience?*

Encourage Application

7. Write "Even if . . . I will . . . " on the board. State that Habakkuk's statement of faith in verses 17–18 takes this stance. Ask, *How would this statement read if it was describing your life and your faith? How can the example of Habakkuk's confrontation with God and his growing faith be of value to us when we face life difficulties?*

8. Read the story about the Andersons in the small article "Case Study" in the *Study Guide*. Call for responses to the question. Ask, *How would Habakkuk's attitude help them?*

9. Close with prayer, thanking God for the Bible and the stories of real people and their struggles with faith that provide an authoritative guide for our lives.

NOTES

1. Hebrew *my stringed.*

2. An appearance of God in visible form.

3. Two to six people each; form groups with duplicate assignments if more than twelve people are in attendance.

Lamentations
1:1–5, 12–22

Background

Lamentations 1—2

Main Idea

The people sorrowed over their great suffering, which had been brought on by their wrongdoing.

Question to Explore

Could it happen again, here?

Teaching Aim

To lead participants to describe the nature of the suffering in this passage and consider its relevance for our day

.AMENTATIONS

Sorrow over a National Tragedy

Lesson Twelve

Weeping in the Night

BIBLE COMMENTS

Understanding the Context

An unbelievable tragedy had befallen the ancient Hebrews. The Babylonians had defeated them and—horror of all horrors—had both profaned and destroyed the temple of Yahweh in Jerusalem. Of those who had survived the destructive military campaign, the ablest had been taken from the land to live in exile among the pagans of other countries under the domination of the Babylonians.

Most modern Americans grieve over losses and tragedies in private or in silence. Not so the ancients: they grieved openly and often loudly. Modern archaeologists sometimes discover ancient "tear bottles"—small bottles of glass or clay, used by professional mourners, hired to wail and cry at funerals. They would fill the small bottles with tears that they had shed on the funeral occasion and present them to survivors as a memento of the grief they had experienced. It is often suggested that the louder the mourning wails, the better.[1]

It is, then, quite understandable that the loss of their temple would bring forth a message of sorrow and mourning laments from God's people. In the Hebrew Bible, the Book of Lamentations is entitled simply *aikah*, or *how*, the first word in the text of the book. The book is placed in the division of the Hebrew Bible called "the Writings" (*Kethuvim*). rather than among the Law (*Torah*) or the Prophets (*Nebiim*). It is one of the five festal scrolls called the *Megilloth*—each read and used in remembering and celebrating (or memorializing) a special or festival day. Lamentations was read on the ninth of the Jewish month of *Ab*, commemorating the day on which the Babylonians destroyed the temple in 587 B.C. and the sorrow caused by that event. Jewish rabbis regularly called the book *Qinoth* or *Dirges*—which usually translates into English as *Laments*, thus "Lamentations."

In our English Bibles (and beginning with Greek Bibles), Lamentations follows the book of the prophet Jeremiah. Sometimes the title in English Bibles is "Lamentations of Jeremiah." Attributing the Book to Jeremiah is likely based on a passage in 2 Chronicles 35:25, which says, "Jeremiah also uttered a lament for Josiah, and all the singing men and singing women have spoken of Josiah in their laments to this day. They made these a custom in Israel; they are recorded in the Laments." Whether or not the "Laments" mentioned in that passage are the same as the lament poems in the Book of Lamentations is an open question. We cannot be certain that Jeremiah authored all or any of the "lament" poems we know as the Book of Lamentations.

The Hebrews had developed a distinctive poetic form to express grief or sorrow. The Hebrew word for this is *Qinah* or *lament*. Ordinary Hebrew poetry has a regular rhythm, equal in accents from line to line. *Qinah* or *lament* poetry, instead, has a limping or uneven rhythm—usually a three-beat line followed by a two-beat line. To the Hebrews this gave a mournful or sorrowful sound. The poems in Lamentations are all in this kind of rhythm. Another distinctive poetry form is found in Lamentations. Four of the five chapters (or poems) are alphabetic acrostics. Chapters 1, 2, and 4 contain twenty-two verses, each beginning with one of the twenty-two letters of the Hebrew alphabet in alphabetic sequence. Chapter 3 has sixty-six verses, with three lines beginning with each of the twenty-two letters of the Hebrew alphabet. Chapter five has twenty-two verses, but the verses do not begin with letters in alphabetic order.

Interpreting the Scriptures

A careful reading of Lamentations 1 shows that at times the worshiper-poet speaks (Lamentations 1:1–11a) and at times the personified city of

Jerusalem seems to speak (Lam. 1:11b–22). Both express heartfelt grief over the ruined condition of the city. Jerusalem was considered the special city in which Yahweh's presence on earth was manifested. No place holds similar religious importance for Christians. Where the temple stood still holds great importance in Judaism, but those feelings were much more intense in Old Testament times.

Grief over the Destroyed City (1:1–15)

1:1. The poet pictured the now-ruined city as a sad shadow of her former glory and power. She who was once a princess and considered great had been reduced to the status of a "vassal"—a servant to other kings and cities—and a widow, grieving over her lost greatness and the loss of worshipers.

1:2. Jerusalem is described in vivid poetic imagery as bereft of friends and "lovers." As a result no one gave her comfort. Friends had betrayed her and become enemies. She was reduced to bitter tears over the treacherous betrayal of friends now become enemies.

1:3. Now in exile, the people of Judah found cruel servitude instead of peace. The intent of the Babylonians in this exile was to create an empire of people without nationalistic ties to a particular geographical area—thus a more controllable and, they hoped, a more integrated empire. Instead, there was a saddened people separated from the land they loved and believed Yahweh had given them. For that lost homeland there was bitter grief.

1:4. The desolate city was overwhelmed by grief. Here "Zion" is used to refer to the entire city of Jerusalem. Technically it is the name of the hill on which the temple was built. It was a place where joyful celebrations of the religious festivals, attended by multitudes, were happy times. Now such times were only memories, marked by mourning, desolation, grief, and bitterness.

1:5. There is a stark contrast between the mastery and prosperity of the enemy and the suffering of the Hebrews taken from the city into exile. But here the cause of the suffering is first introduced: "the multitude of her transgressions." The word translated "transgressions" is the Hebrew word for *deliberate and intentional sinful rebellion against Yahweh.* The Hebrews had every reason to know better, but they sinned against God in spite of that knowledge. Such sinful rebellion could not be atoned for by the offering of burnt sacrifices. The sinner must cast himself or herself on the mercy of God, pleading for forgiveness with a truly penitent spirit. That the Hebrews had failed to do. The exile was the response to their failure to repent. True repentance involves not only sorrow but change. Perhaps the sorrow was there, but the change was not.

1:6–11a. The lament over the city of Jerusalem continues in these verses, as the city is described as a reckless and decadent young woman, wandering from the way of faithfulness, eventually falling from her position as a majestic city into the hands of her foes, who delighted in her downfall. Her failings and wanton ways had resulted in mocking taunts from her enemies, who were oppressing her people.

1:11b–12. Here the author shifts to the first person, with the now rebellious city of Jerusalem speaking: "See how worthless I have become." No one seemed to care about her degraded condition. Passersby were asked whether they had ever seen such sorrow and anguish before, so great was the distress Jerusalem and its people faced. The first half of verse 12 will be familiar to many because John Stainer used it in his magnificent musical work, "The Crucifixion," to describe the uncaring crowd who witnessed the crucifixion of Jesus. The verse addresses the callous and uncaring response of people in all ages to the suffering and needs of others, and especially the failure to respond to the sacrificial love of God ultimately expressed in Christ on the cross.

Sin, Suffering, and Judgment (1:13–15)

Fire in the bones is a figure expressing the ultimate in pain. The judgment of Yahweh on the sinful city brought great suffering. Remember that in the thought of Old Testament people Jerusalem was the earthly dwelling place of Yahweh. Now they were separated from the God who cared for them. The Hebrews were, by human or earthly standards, weak and almost a "nobody" nation. The judgment God sent on them got their attention, something the prophetic messages had failed to accomplish.

It is not true to say that suffering always comes as a result of sin. Sometimes it does, though, and when it does it can make one aware of his or her sin and call the sinner to repentance. This is clearly set out in verse 14. When "transgressions are made a yoke" (author's translation), they are laid on the sinner to be carried. The heavy load of punishment brought on by deliberate rebellion against Yahweh certainly got the attention of the willfully rebellious nation. The graphic poetic description of a people subdued by a strong and cruel enemy clearly depicts the fall and devastation of Jerusalem by the Neo-Babylonian forces in 587 B.C. As grapes were crushed to a pulp in a winepress, so the nation had been destroyed completely.

Jerusalem's Response to Divine Judgment (1:16–22)

1:16. Sorrow was the first response to the tragedy that had overtaken the city. No comforter was to be found. It is tempting to associate sorrow with repentance. Sometimes they go together, but often they do not. Repentance includes a willingness and determination to change. In our culture many people are sorry they were caught in wrongdoing, but they do not acknowledge that the wrongdoing led to their being caught. The same was almost certainly true for the ancient Hebrews. At this point the poem contains no indication that their sorrow was leading to change. Repentance refers to sorrow that leads to change.

1:17. No comfort was to be found for the devastated city. The surrounding cities and nations did not reach out to give solace. In the world of the ancient Middle East, small states competed with one another for power and even for security. In her time of great need, none reached out to Jerusalem. They were selfishly looking out for themselves. Jerusalem was one of their foes. In fact, Jerusalem had become a "dirty word" to them. As we might put it today, *No one would give her the time of day.* Often the sinner revels in the company of fellow sinners, but in the end the sinner stands alone with no one to support or comfort.

1:18. Finally the truth began to dawn on Jerusalem: *I am a sinner, and all of this tragedy and suffering of captivity has come about because of rebellion against Yahweh.*

1:19–20. Then Israel realized she had been trusting earthly "lovers"— other nations and peoples—for security, but they proved to be worse than useless. They provided no comfort. There was only bereavement and sorrowful anguish.

1:21–22. This poem concludes with a prayer for the punishment of the Hebrews' enemies (and those who once were friends but who proved in the end to be enemies). *They knew how I was hurting,* Jerusalem said to Yahweh, *but they did nothing.* The poem concludes with a prayer that Yahweh would do to those enemies just what he had done to Jerusalem—visit them with total destruction.

A second alphabetic poem is found in chapter two. It contains a vivid picture of the devastation visited on Judah and Jerusalem. The righteous anger of Yahweh is described in vibrant poetry, pointing out both the underlying causes and the extent of the destruction visited on Jerusalem. In this poem the totality of the destruction visited on Jerusalem is pictured even more clearly than in chapter 1.

Focusing on the Meaning

Suffering is one of the major themes in the wisdom literature in the Old Testament. After all, God's people, Israel, had suffered the loss of freedom, a homeland, and even their temple, which was the focus of their religious life. Mistakenly, but humanly, they had felt secure as Yahweh's people. They believed that their ancestry made them secure. They had not yet learned the lesson that each person is responsible to God. There was and is no "group" salvation. Never draw the conclusion that you are safe and secure because of your association with or even "belonging" to a church. Your own personal faith and relationship with God is what matters.

Suffering can embitter one and drive him or her away from God. Or it can lead one to self-examination in depth and total honesty and then result in a deeper faith and a closer walk with God. Whether we "deserve" suffering, we can learn from it and be drawn to a closer relationship with God.

Most of us can hardly comprehend the suffering of the Hebrews in the exile. The Babylonian king, Nebuchadnezzar (also translated Nebuchadrezzar), completely conquered the nation of Judah. He took all the upper classes and the skilled workers and their families to the region of Babylon. Probably there were at least two motives. A people separated from their homes and country will less likely start a rebellion against their overlord. Note that he left behind only the peasant population. Without leadership they would not likely revolt. Also, taking the skilled people and the upper classes would enhance, both socially and economically, Babylon and the region around his capital city. Deportation was likely a common practice at the time on the part of a conqueror who was building an empire. By modern standards it was cruel and inhumane—but it worked, at least for a time.

The ancient Hebrews had many prayers of repentance in their Psalter, but these had not led them to repent. As noted, repentance involves change. If there is no change, there is no repentance. The practices of worship are good and are commended, but if there is no personal involvement that has its impact on how we live, it is so much ritual and no more.

Many Baptists would argue that we have no ritual, but most of us do. We follow the same, or a similar, order of worship each Sunday. We can become so comfortable with it that often we simply "go through the motions" and never subject our lives to examination that must come when we realize that we are face to face with an Almighty God. When we do that, the likelihood of true repentance and change is greatly increased.

Let us not make the same mistake that the ancient Hebrews made. When you worship, realize that you are in the presence of the Almighty Creator of heaven and earth. Subject your life to an examination in the light of God's word and God's presence. I promise you: some changes will be in order.

TEACHING PLANS

Teaching Plan—Varied Learning Activities

Connect with Life

1. Before the session, locate two or three pictures (actual photos from magazines articles, printed from the internet, etc.) that depict utter devastation. These can include pictures from war areas, terrorism targets, tornado or hurricane aftermath, or other natural disasters. Try not to choose photos that are quickly recognizable (such as the New York Twin Towers aftermath).

2. Divide the class into two or three groups of six people or fewer, giving each group one of the pictures. Ask everyone to look closely at their pictures and develop an elaborate story that describes what has just happened. Have them include an account of what happened, who was affected, how they were affected, where they are now, etc. After giving each group about five minutes, have them take turns sharing their fictitious stories with the rest of the class. Use these stories to

make the transition into the lesson by explaining that the backdrop to today's session is Jerusalem's response to her complete desolation at the hands of a ruthless Babylonian king.

Guide Bible Study

3. Invite someone to summarize "Introducing Lamentations" in the *Study Guide* (perhaps enlist the person in advance). Add information from "Understanding the Context" in this *Teaching Guide* to introduce the Book of Lamentations further.

4. Enlist a member in advance who will do an expressive reading of Lamentations 1:1–5. Select someone who will really provide a dramatic flare. Welcome everyone to today's reading of a poetic work. Share with the class that the enlisted person is going to be reading an account of the mournful cries of a desecrated city. Point out that Lamentations 1 is written in a very distinct poetic style. Share that it is actually an acrostic poem, with each of the twenty-two verses beginning with the next letter in the Hebrew alphabet. Ask each person to make a list of all the problems that are expressed in this passage as the account is being read. One by one, have members share items from their lists, and use the suggestions to write and display a master list. Lead a brief discussion on the plight of the people in the story. Use information in the *Study Guide* and in "Bible Comments" in this *Teaching Guide* to explain the verses.

5. Read Lamentations 1:12–22. Ask class members to raise their hands as you are reading each time they hear the words "I," "my" or "me." Point out that the people's focus is still dangerously on themselves and not on pleasing God. Use information in the *Study Guide* and in "Bible Comments" in this *Teaching Guide* to explain the verses. Invite participants to share about a time in their life when they felt God was allowing them to suffer through some difficult situations because they were disregarding his will for their lives.

Encourage Application

6. Divide the class into two groups, giving each group a slip of paper with one of the following two assignments (download from

www.baptistwaypress.org). Be sure to have the identified supplies available. Groups should not be larger than six people. If you have a large class, you might choose to duplicate these assignments and have multiple groups doing the same tasks.

Group 1: Using the magazines provided, cut out pictures of things that depict the spiritual demise of people in today's society. Glue these items on the provided poster board to form a "collage of despair." Select someone in your group to explain your creation to the rest of the class.

Group 2: Songs often tell stories about the realities of life and daily struggles and hardships. Write two stanzas of a song that describe things in today's society that could bring God's punishment on the world. You may choose to use the tune of another song as the basis from which to develop your own. Select a person (or people) in your group to sing your new creation to the rest of the class.

7. After all the groups have shared their creative insights into the plight of today's world, ask the following question: *So, do you think what we just read about in Lamentations could happen again today? How does Lamentations speak to us today?* Invite responses. Point out that the first step in moving our nation toward what God desires is for individual people to commit themselves to living their lives according to God's will. Encourage class members to spend one or two minutes of silence, asking themselves the following question (*Study Guide* question 4): "What do I need to repent of before I can really be right with God?" During this time of silence, have members talk with God about that area in their life. After providing some time for individual personal confession, close with prayer.

Teaching Plan—Lecture and Questions

Connect with Life

1. Remind class members of the introductory story in the *Study Guide* of the writer's family vacation. Ask the following questions:
   a. What made the *War of the Worlds* exhibit so significant?

   b. The *War of the Worlds* set was imaginary. Has anyone in our class seen real devastation first hand? What did you see?

   c. How did this devastation make you feel?

Use responses to these questions to explain that the backdrop for today's lesson is Jerusalem's response to her own complete desolation at the hands of a ruthless Babylonian king.

Guide Bible Study

2. Summarize "Introducing Lamentations" in the *Study Guide* and "Understanding the Context" in this *Teaching Guide* to introduce the Book of Lamentations.

3. Display a poster with the following outline of the lesson:

Weeping in the Night
Before and After Snapshots (1:1–5)
Crying Out for Attention (1:12–16)
A Final Plea (1:17–22)

---

4. Enlist a volunteer to read Lamentations 1:1–5. Explain that although these verses talk about a woman, they are actually referring to the city of Jerusalem. Assign half the class to listen for what the city used to be like and half to listen for what the city was like then. Explain that this first section is entitled, "Before and After Snapshots." Invite someone to explain what significance the title has to this group of verses. Have members find and share aloud all of the ways the verses depict the woman *before* God's judgment. List responses on a chalkboard/markerboard. Next, have members do the same with how the woman is depicted *after* God's judgment. List these responses beside the others.

5. Read Lamentations 1:12–22. Ask the class to listen for the descriptions of the situation of the city. Use information from the *Study Guide* and "Bible Comments" in this *Teaching Guide* to point out the following aspects of these verses:

   a. Jerusalem felt no one cared about her situation. Invite volunteers to share about a time when they felt this way.

---

   b. Explain the idea of the net in Lamentations 1:13. Refer also
      to Job 19:6. Point out that the reference is to the idea of God
      capturing them, enslaving them, and putting them under
      complete subjection.
   c. Use the discussion in the *Study Guide* about the term "yoke" to
      explain briefly what the term means. Ask whether anyone has
      ever seen a yoke in person.
   d. Ask why the "yoke" was an appropriate term to be used in
      Jerusalem's situation.
   e. Inquire whether class members have had anything in their
      lives they would consider to be a yoke of oppression.

Encourage Application

6. Ask the following questions: *How do these verses from Lamentations 1
   speak to you? What relevance do you think they have for us? What things
   do you see happening in the world today that might lead you to believe
   that God could once again pour out his judgment?* Make a list of these
   items on the board as members share their ideas.

7. After accumulating the list, explain that in order for the world to
   get right with God and avoid God's harsh punishment, individual
   people will need to commit themselves to living their lives according
   to God's will. Encourage class members to spend two or three minutes of silence, asking themselves the following question (question 4
   in the *Study Guide)*: "What do I need to repent of before I can really
   be right with God?" During this time of silence, encourage members
   to talk with God about that area in their life. After providing some
   time for individual personal confession, close with prayer.

NOTES

1. Unless otherwise indicated, all Scripture quotes in lessons 12–13 on
   Lamentations are from the New Revised Standard Version.

Background

Lamentations 3

Main Idea

God loves us in spite of our sins and offers forgiveness and restoration when we return to him.

Question to Explore

How can we and our church encourage people to return to the Lord?

Teaching Aim

To lead participants to consider ways for encouraging people to return to the Lord

LAMENTATIONS

Sorrow over a National Tragedy

Lesson Thirteen

God's Steadfast Love

BIBLE COMMENTS

Understanding the Context

As with the Scriptures in the previous lesson on Lamentations, this chapter is a lament crying out in open grief for their lost homeland by the Hebrews in exile after the Babylonians had devastated Jerusalem and all of Judah in 587 B.C. Also as noted in lesson twelve, the Babylonian policy was to move any possible leaders of the defeated people away from their homeland. One goal of this practice was to break the ties people felt to their native land. They would more likely rise up in revolt for their ancestral homes than for another land on which they had been resettled. Too, taking the wealthy, upper class people to Babylon would build up the economy and power of the capital of the Babylonian Empire.

No identifiable single incident called forth this poem of lament. It is a carefully and beautifully constructed alphabetic acrostic poem, and a somewhat unusual one. It contains sixty-six verses. Three verses begin with each letter of the Hebrew alphabet. That is, each of verses 1, 2, and 3 begins with *aleph*; each of verses 4, 5, and 6 begins with a *beth*. And so on the poem goes through the alphabet. Here and in the other alphabetic poems of Lamentations the position of two of the letters (*pe* and *ayin*) is reversed from the usual order.

In reading and teaching this lesson, remember that a great tragedy had befallen Jerusalem, its temple, and all those who loved and worshiped Yahweh. The Babylonian armies had not only captured Jerusalem, their holy city, but they also had carried away all the treasures and valuable appointments in the temple. The Babylonians then completely demolished the temple structure. The religiously faithful of Judah had suffered a threefold tragedy: they lost their homes, their freedom, and the temple, which they believed to be the earthly dwelling of Yahweh, their God. With this in mind, we can better understand the poignant poem of grief and lament we consider today.

This poem is a very personal lament in which the writer, be he Jeremiah or some unknown, worked through his grief. He expressed his sorrow over his trials and afflictions and then his resignation to them, accepting them. As the lament continues, he repented and finally reaffirmed his trust in God. There is here a graphic and beautifully expressed journey from deep depression and sorrow to affirmation of faith in God.

Interpreting the Scriptures

Affliction Comes from God (3:1–3)

In three lines or verses, each beginning with the Hebrew letter *aleph*, the tone of this lament begins with a personal testimony of one who has experienced the wrath of a righteous God and who feels imprisoned by it. There is no escape, for the punishment is from the Almighty. It was not unusual for those in exile, as this writer probably was, to understand that the major cause for the exile of Judah was a divinely sent punishment on the nation. The exiles felt this punishment every day, all day long.

Despair So Deep It Was Like Death (3:4–6)

How better to describe deep despair than to use terms describing physical pain and distress? It is likened to broken bones and wasted, shriveled flesh and skin. The picture is one of bitterness, trouble, and darkness as if one had been dead for a long time.

Hopelessness Abounds When No Escape Is Seen (3:7–9)

The exiles faced the restraint of high walls and heavy chains with an attitude of hopelessness. Their cries for help and prayers for deliverance were going unanswered. Escape seemed impossible. The way is described as extremely crooked and blocked by stones cut for that purpose, not just stones scattered on the pathway of escape.

There is no historical record of the Hebrew exiles in Babylon being physically held by chains in walled prisons. It is likely that these descriptions are figurative expressions of how the exiles felt, kept by the Babylonians without the possibility of returning to their homeland.

Despair! (3:10–18)

The despair of the poet deepens. Bitterness and awareness of danger fill his heart. He can find neither peace nor happiness.

Several graphic analogies describe the despair brought by the exile. He likens his situation to being stalked by a bear or a lion and to being the target for the soldier with the bow. He is filled with bitterness and can find no peace. His considered conclusion is this: "Gone is my glory and my expectation from the LORD" (Lamentations 3:18, author's translation). He appears to have given up on God.

But All Hope Is Not Lost! (3:19–21)

Just when the future seemed overwhelmingly bleak, a ray of hope came. When thinking about his situation, even all its bitterness spurred his mind to consider the reality of God—and that brought hope. The poet's bitterness of mind and spirit is described in terms of wormwood—a shrub with a very bitter taste—and gall, a substance known for its bitterness as well. But in the midst of his despair he thought of God. With God, hope or any other positive is possible. True, God is not mentioned in this verse, but as we read the next verse, it is clear what the basis for his hope was.

God's Faithfulness, Mercy, and Trustworthiness Regardless of Our Actions (3:22–24)

In what is probably the most beautiful and often remembered passage in this lesson, the despairing soul realized that he had been selling God short. God had been there all the time.

We can translate verse 22 like this: "The covenant love of Yahweh is why we are not consumed; because his compassions (or mercies) do not fail" (author's translation). The word here translated "covenant love" (in the NRSV "steadfast love") is one of the strongest and most meaningful words in all of the Hebrew Bible—*hesed.*

The word pictures the love Yahweh pledged to his people in the covenant made at Mount Sinai (Exodus 19—24). This covenant pledged Yahweh's continuing loving care for his people. But the condition was faithful obedience to Yahweh's covenant laws, which the people pledged to follow. They must fulfill their part, the conditions to which they agreed. They could count on Yahweh to be faithful—the emphasis of the Hebrew is that morning by morning—"every morning"—God would be there for them. The people had failed miserably in keeping their part of the covenant agreement. But as they looked to God with repentance, in his compassion or mercy he would forgive and reclaim his people, even in the land of exile.

To paraphrase the Hebrew of verse 24: "That Yahweh is my portion (or share or inheritance) is affirmed by my innermost being; therefore I can hope in him." Knowing a God who can be totally and eternally trusted is one of the great gifts in our religion. The Hebrews and their contemporaries lived in a world of many gods, but these gods were capricious and unpredictable, thus untrustworthy. The Hebrews had much for which to be grateful—as do we.

The Need for Repentance (3:25–30)

The guilty must accept the punishment justly sent and wait quietly for the salvation Yahweh would surely send. Waiting before God is important. Accepting the punishment that God sends is a necessary prelude to restoration and blessings. God's salvation is assured, but there must first come the penitent spirit that accepts the punishment God sends.

Three graphic figures are used in 3:28–30 to describe the needed repentance. (1) To "sit alone in silence" (Lam. 3:28) describes one who is waiting before God, not making excuses, simply waiting. (2) "To put one's mouth to the dust" (3:29) pictures one prostrate before God, accepting God's judgment without excuses or objection. (3) Giving a "cheek to the smiter" (3:30) and thus accepting insults pictures one who acknowledges his wrongdoing, without making excuses, accepting whatever punishment is sent.

The Marvelous Kind of Love God Has for Us (3:31–33)

We worship a loving and forgiving God, one who does not find any pleasure in meting out punishment on his people. The righteous nature of God demands that he reject and punish sinful rebellion. Yet the purpose of God's punishment is not to cause harm and grief. Rather it is done with compassion, directed toward reclaiming the rebelling one to the family of a loving God.

The key word in this section is the "steadfast love" that God uses to reclaim the wayward ones. His love is a *covenant love*, a love that leads him to have compassion for the wayward when human emotion would argue for rejection of the wayward. Even to the wayward, God offers love instead of the pain and grief of rejection. Although we often fall short of being fully what God wills and hopes for us to be, his compassionate, forgiving love redeems us and gives us hope instead of despair.

God Sees and Knows Our Condition (3:34–36)

These verses sound a further note of hope. When prisoners are mistreated—and this was long before anything near the modern concern that even the worst of prisoners have rights and must be treated in humane ways—the all-seeing Yahweh sees and knows.

God Is a Just and Righteous Judge (3:37–39)

God's punishment as the consequence of our sins is altogether just—perhaps more merciful than merely just. Although people often complain, there is no basis for complaints to such a righteous and just God.

We Must Look Within (3:40–41)

With this passage and through the remainder of the chapter, the author speaks in the first person, identifying himself with the sorrowing and often complaining people. People, then as now, need to do some serious self-examination as they stand before God. The result will be more self-searching and less complaining; more confession than blaming God for whatever in life we want to complain about.

The ancient Hebrews had assumed too much. They were the chosen nation, bound to Yahweh in a covenant relationship, dating back to the

Exodus experience at Sinai (Exodus 19—24). It seems that many of the Hebrews of this time thought that they had inherited the assurance of God's blessings because of that experience. They had to learn that each generation (and each person) must make a personal commitment to God, confessing their sins and taking upon themselves the responsibilities of loyal obedience to the covenanting God their ancestors had worshiped and honored.

Is God Indeed Hidden? (3:42–54)

Reasons for feeling great distance from God are explained in these verses. These reasons are transgression and rebellion that are yet unforgiven because there has been no confession and repentance. As a result there is a sense of being distant from God. In experiencing God's judgment on them for their sins, they feel that God is hidden behind a cloud so that even their prayers cannot penetrate to his ear. Their enemies have brought horrors and desolation on Israel. Tears have poured down like torrents, but the tears are clearly tears of grief and not of repentance. The sense of national anguish over their defeat and exile was overwhelming. The realization of their situation finally called forth repentance: "I am lost" (Lam. 3:54).

Reaching Out to God (3:55–58)

Following the sinner's cry, "I am lost," the sinner heard this message from God: "Do not fear" (3:57). Sometimes we must come to the end of our rope before we can come to God in faith and trust. These verses describe that experience. Only when we acknowledge that God is indeed with us and in control can we proceed without fear.

A Cry for God to Deal with the Enemies (3:59–66)

A human response to oppression is the desire for revenge. These final verses of this chapter express a strong desire for God to visit this oppressive enemy with punishment for avenging the wrongs done to Israel. Remember that this is in the Old Testament. The Hebrews had not arrived at the higher teaching of Jesus, who requires that we forgive even as God forgives us and that we love our enemies as well as our friends.

Focusing on the Meaning

Life is often filled with trouble, many times with tragedies we cannot understand. We want to shake a fist toward God and cry: *Why has this happened to me?* This grief-filled poem depicts the Hebrews doing just that. Those who had been faithful worshipers of Yahweh could not understand why conquest, destruction, and exile were happening to them. Questioning God is not in itself sinful—as long as we let God answer. Crisis and tragedy can be the way of opening us to God and establishing a deeper and more meaningful relationship with him.

How do we respond to suffering, oppression, and various difficulties? We can respond by hating those who appear to be the perpetrators of our difficulties or sufferings. But Jesus taught us to love them and to pray for them. We can try to gain enough power to take revenge and "get even" with them. But Jesus' words from the cross instruct us to forgive instead of condemn.

It is important that we come to a clear understanding of ourselves. The Scriptures tell us that we are all sinful (Romans 3:23). Our "good" deeds are likened to filthy rags (Isaiah 64:6). We sometimes develop a feeling that God owes us something. Actually we owe God everything. Instead of lamenting our troubles, we need to thank God for his grace and mercy.

Isn't it remarkable that God loves us in spite of all our sinful thoughts and deeds, failures, and mistakes? The Old Testament writer could not know—but we do—the fullness of the great forgiving love that led to Calvary. The greatest tragedy of any life is failing to respond to that forgiving love that led to Calvary.

TEACHING PLANS

Teaching Plan—Varied Learning Activities

Connect with Life

1. Before the session, go through a newspaper and cut out five or six stories of people living locally or around the world who have endured

some type of calamity. As members arrive, distribute the articles and ask them to be prepared to share briefly about the articles' content. (Or you could just ask people to name such calamities in step 3.)

2. Begin the session by asking for a volunteer to share about a difficult situation that he or she is currently going through or has recently endured. Depending on the individuals in your class, and perhaps situations about which you are already aware, it may be better to enlist the person in advance. If time allows, you may choose to call on several individuals to share.

3. Call on the pre-enlisted members to share with the entire group about the newspaper articles they have read. Use this opportunity to point out that hardship and catastrophe occur universally. There is no respect for age, socioeconomic group, or religious affiliation. Relate that there is really no question *whether* difficult times will come into our lives. The only question is *how* we will respond to those difficulties.

Guide Bible Study

4. Lead the class to share how they see the world responding to life's calamities. Record responses on a markerboard or chalkboard. Point out that although it is not always the case, at least some of the awful things we see happening in the world are a direct result of sin. Explain that we are going to be looking at an event that happened more than 2,500 years ago as a result of the collective sin of a group of people. Ask members to be considering the following questions as they study together:
   a. Could the sin of our nation cause similar consequences today?
   b. If so, what will keep us from going down the same path as Jerusalem?

5. Divide the class into three groups, assigning each group one of the following sets of verses: Lamentations 3:1–3; 3:4–6; 3:7–9. Give groups a few minutes to read their verses and collectively write a modern-day paraphrase of their sections. Once everyone has finished, have a spokesperson from each group first read the assigned verses out of Lamentations and then read the modern paraphrased version they have created. Use the content from the Bible study material in

the *Study Guide* and in "Bible Comments" in this *Teaching Guide* to describe what is happening during the first section of verses, welcoming any class input. Be sure to point out the magnitude of what had happened to the people of Jerusalem and the fact that the adversities they had endured were a direct result of their sin.

6. Have a volunteer read Lamentations 3:19–25. Ask the following questions and allow time for responses:
    a. What kind of change has taken place from the tone of the first verses in this chapter to the ones we just read?
    b. What do you think caused this change?
    c. What do you think about the poet's expressing his unhappiness to the Lord in the earlier verses? Do you think it was all right to do so?
    d. Do you think it's a good practice to look back at the down times in our lives? Why or why not?

7. Read Lamentations 3:26–41, asking the class to listen for steps in the process of returning to the Lord. After the reading, give a few moments for the class to identify the steps to themselves. Then call for responses and guide the discussion. Have paper and pencils available in case they are needed. Consider the following for the list:
    a. Wait quietly (3:26).
    b. Get right with God while you're still young (3:27).
    c. Listen for the Lord's direction (3:28).
    d. Humble oneself (3:29).
    e. Accept one's punishment (3:30).
    f. Recognize God's benevolent spirit (3:31–36).
    g. Recognize hardship resulting from sin as God's purposeful discipline (3:37–39).
    h. Examine one's own heart and motives (3:40).
    i. Return to God (3:40–41).

Encourage Application

8. Using the same three teams from the earlier exercise (step 5), have each group select one representative to come to the markerboard/chalkboard. Give each of the volunteers a marker or chalk, and instruct them that they will be competing to see who can draw the

best picture of a particular scene. Tell them that all three will be drawing at the same time, and they will need to each listen as their own group members instruct them on what to include in the picture. They will need to follow their group's instructions precisely, only including things that they are told. Let everyone know that they will be able to start as soon as you tell them what they will be drawing, and that this will not be a competition for speed, but for the content of the picture. Once the contestants are ready, announce that they need to draw a person praying. When all three groups are finished, have each describe what they have drawn and why they included certain aspects. Ask what difficulties they encountered. If it is not mentioned, ask whether focusing only on the voices of their own team was a challenge. Use this exercise to point out two important things in today's lesson:

a. The only way to get through the difficult times in life is through prayer. Verse 29 actually indicates that a person should "bury his face in the dust" (NIV), which refers to laying ourselves out prostrate on the ground in full submission to God. Ask, *Did any of our pictures we just drew have us humbling ourselves to that point?*

b. In order to get through adversity and move back on the path the Lord has for us, we will need to focus intently on the voice of God, blocking out the input we are getting from all around us.

9. Close the session by asking for responses to questions 3 and 4 under "Questions" in the *Study Guide.* The two questions are as follows: "What rebellion do I see happening in society that could bring God's harsh discipline?" "What could my church do to encourage people to return to the Lord?"

10. Encourage class members to spend one or two minutes of silent prayer, considering question 5 from "Questions": "What is one area in my own life over which I need to surrender control to God?" During this time of silence, have members talk with God about that one area in their life. After providing some time for individual personal confession, close with prayer.

Teaching Plan—Lecture and Questions

Connect with Life

1. Begin the session by asking for a volunteer to tell about a difficult situation that he or she is currently going through or has recently endured. Depending on the individuals in your class, and perhaps situations about which you are already aware, it may be better to enlist the person in advance. If time allows, you may choose to call on several individuals to share.

2. Use the response(s) to remind members of the plight in which Jerusalem found herself. Also point out that although the situation that Lamentations describes happened somewhere around 587 B.C.—more than 2,500 years ago—we can still relate to the experience of adversity and even catastrophe in our lives today. Explain that you are going to be exploring together the poet's personal response to the things that had happened to Jerusalem, and then you will be contemplating what that response says to our society today.

Guide Bible Study

3. Display a poster with the following outline of the lesson:

> ### God's Steadfast Love
> Sharing Sorrow (3:1–9)
> Proclaiming Hope (3:19–25)
> Suggesting a Solution (3:26–30)
> Recognizing God's Desire (3:31–41)

4. Enlist a volunteer to read Lamentations 3:1–9 while the class listens for the difficulties expressed. Explain that this first section is entitled, "Sharing Sorrow." Point out that in these initial comments in chapter 3, the poet is still in the mode of complaining about the terrible circumstances the people have had to endure at the hands of the Babylonian armies. Ask members to identify some of the specific complaints. As people share ideas, record the responses on a markerboard or chalkboard. Allow time for conversation, as appropriate.

Use the *Study Guide* and "Bible Comments" in this *Teaching Guide* to provide more detailed information as needed.

5. Read Lamentations 3:19–27 aloud while the class listens for positive ideas in these verses. Use the *Study Guide* and "Bible Comments" in this *Teaching Guide* to explain these verses. Be certain to pay particular attention to the following ideas or thought questions.

   a. How can remembering difficult times sometimes serve to strengthen our faith?

   b. Have someone read Psalm 16:5–6. Discuss how the Old Testament term "portion" was used, and relate that to Lamentations 3:24.

   c. What do you think about the poet's expressing unhappiness to the Lord in the earlier section of verses? Was it all right to do?

6. Refer to Lamentations 3:28–41, and have the class read these verses to themselves to identify specific directions regarding returning to God. Call for responses, and write them on a markerboard or chalkboard. (For ideas, see step 7 in the other teaching plan.) Use this list and information in the *Study Guide* and "Bible Comments" in this *Teaching Guide* to lead further discussion on this final set of verses.

Encourage Application

7. Point out that this Scripture called people to return to the Lord. Ask: *How does that apply to our day? What specific things could we do to help encourage people to return to the Lord?* Allow adequate time for thoughtful responses before following up with a similar question: *What practical things could our church do to encourage people (inside or outside the congregation) to turn to the Lord?* Make a list of these items on the board as members share their ideas.

8. Encourage class members to spend one or two minutes of silence, thinking about question 5 from "Questions" in the *Study Guide:* "What is one area in my life over which I need to surrender control to God?" After providing some time for individual personal confession, close with prayer.

How to Order More Bible Study Materials

It's easy! Just fill in the following information. For additional Bible study materials, see www.baptistwaypress.org or get a complete order form of available materials by calling 1-866-249-1799 or e-mailing baptistway@bgct.org.

Title of item	Price	Quantity	Cost
This Issue:			
Job, Ecclesiastes, Habakkuk, Lamentations: Dealing with Hard Times—Study Guide (BWP001016)	$2.75	_____	_____
Job, Ecclesiastes, Habakkuk, Lamentations: Dealing with Hard Times—Large Print Study Guide (BWP001017)	$2.85	_____	_____
Job, Ecclesiastes, Habakkuk, Lamentations: Dealing with Hard Times—Teaching Guide (BWP001018)	$3.25	_____	_____
Additional Issues Available:			
Genesis 12—50: Family Matters—Study Guide (BWP000034)	$1.95	_____	_____
Genesis 12—50: Family Matters—Large Print Study Guide (BWP000032)	$1.95	_____	_____
Genesis 12—50: Family Matters—Teaching Guide (BWP000035)	$2.45	_____	_____
Leviticus, Numbers, Deuteronomy—Study Guide (BWP000053)	$2.35	_____	_____
Leviticus, Numbers, Deuteronomy—Large Print Study Guide (BWP000052)	$2.35	_____	_____
Leviticus, Numbers, Deuteronomy—Teaching Guide (BWP000054)	$2.95	_____	_____
Joshua, Judges—Study Guide (BWP000047)	$2.35	_____	_____
Joshua, Judges—Large Print Study Guide (BWP000046)	$2.35	_____	_____
Joshua, Judges—Teaching Guide (BWP000048)	$2.95	_____	_____
1 and 2 Samuel—Study Guide (BWP000002)	$2.35	_____	_____
1 and 2 Samuel—Large Print Study Guide (BWP000001)	$2.35	_____	_____
1 and 2 Samuel—Teaching Guide (BWP000003)	$2.95	_____	_____
Psalms and Proverbs: Songs and Sayings of Faith—Study Guide (BWP001000)	$2.75	_____	_____
Psalms and Proverbs: Songs and Sayings of Faith—Large Print Study Guide (BWP001001)	$2.85	_____	_____
Psalms and Proverbs: Songs and Sayings of Faith—Teaching Guide (BWP001002)	$3.25	_____	_____
Jesus in the Gospel of Mark—Study Guide (BWP000066)	$1.95	_____	_____
Jesus in the Gospel of Mark—Large Print Study Guide (BWP000065)	$1.95	_____	_____
Jesus in the Gospel of Mark—Teaching Guide (BWP000067)	$2.45	_____	_____
Luke: Journeying to the Cross—Study Guide (BWP000057)	$2.35	_____	_____
Luke: Journeying to the Cross—Large Print Study Guide (BWP000056)	$2.35	_____	_____
Luke: Journeying to the Cross—Teaching Guide (BWP000058)	$2.95	_____	_____
The Gospel of John: The Word Became Flesh—Study Guide (BWP001008)	$2.75	_____	_____
The Gospel of John: The Word Became Flesh—Large Print Study Guide (BWP001009)	$2.85	_____	_____
The Gospel of John: The Word Became Flesh—Teaching Guide (BWP001010)	$3.25	_____	_____
Acts: Toward Being a Missional Church—Study Guide (BWP001013)	$2.75	_____	_____
Acts: Toward Being a Missional Church—Large Print Study Guide (BWP001014)	$2.85	_____	_____
Acts: Toward Being a Missional Church—Teaching Guide (BWP001015)	$3.25	_____	_____
2 Corinthians: Taking Ministry Personally—Study Guide (BWP000008)	$2.35	_____	_____
2 Corinthians: Taking Ministry Personally—Large Print Study Guide (BWP000007)	$2.35	_____	_____
2 Corinthians: Taking Ministry Personally —Teaching Guide (BWP000009)	$2.95	_____	_____

1, 2 Timothy, Titus, Philemon—*Study Guide* (BWP000092)	$2.75	_____	_____
1, 2 Timothy, Titus, Philemon—*Large Print Study Guide* (BWP000091)	$2.85	_____	_____
1, 2 Timothy, Titus, Philemon—*Teaching Guide* (BWP000093)	$3.25	_____	_____
Hebrews and James—*Study Guide* (BWP000037)	$1.95	_____	_____
Hebrews and James—*Teaching Guide* (BWP000038)	$2.45	_____	_____
Revelation—*Study Guide* (BWP000084)	$2.35	_____	_____
Revelation—*Large Print Study Guide* (BWP000083)	$2.35	_____	_____
Revelation—*Teaching Guide* (BWP000085)	$2.95	_____	_____

Coming for use beginning September 2007

Romans: What God Is Up To—*Study Guide* (BWP001019)	$2.95	_____	_____
Romans: What God Is Up To—*Large Print Study Guide* (BWP001020)	$3.15	_____	_____
Romans: What God Is Up To—*Teaching Guide* (BWP001021)	$3.45	_____	_____

Cost of items (Order value) _____
Processing fee (1% of Cost of Items) _____
Shipping charges (see chart*) _____
TOTAL _____

Standard (UPS/Mail) Shipping Charges*	
Order Value	Shipping charge
$.01—$9.99	$5.00
$10.00—$19.99	$6.00
$20.00—$39.99	$7.00
$40.00—$79.99	$8.00
$80.00—$99.99	$11.00
$100.00—$129.99	$13.00
$130.00—$149.99	$17.00
$150.00—$199.99	$20.00
$200.00—$299.99	$25.00
$300.00 and up	10% of order value

*Plus, applicable taxes for individuals and other taxable entities (not churches) within Texas will be added. Please call 1-866-249-1799 if the exact amount is needed prior to ordering.

Please allow three weeks for standard delivery. For express shipping service: Call 1-866-249-1799 for information on additional charges.

YOUR NAME _____ PHONE _____

YOUR CHURCH _____ DATE ORDERED _____

MAILING ADDRESS _____

CITY _____ STATE ____ ZIP CODE ____

MAIL this form with your check for the total amount to
BAPTISTWAY PRESS, Baptist General Convention of Texas,
333 North Washington, Dallas, TX 75246-1798
(Make checks to "Baptist Executive Board.")

OR, **FAX** your order anytime to: 214-828-5376, and we will bill you.

OR, **CALL** your order toll-free: 1-866-249-1799
(M-Th 8:30 a.m.-8:30 p.m.; Fri 8:30 a.m.-5:00 p.m.), and we will bill you.

OR, **E-MAIL** your order to our internet e-mail address:
baptistway@bgct.org, and we will bill you.

OR, **ORDER ONLINE** at www.baptistwaypress.org.

We look forward to receiving your order! Thank you!